Royal Fireworks   Language Arts   by Michael Clay Thompson

CAESAR'S ENGLISH

CLASSICAL EDUCATION EDITION

PART ONE
APRIL 2012

Michael Clay Thompson
Myriam Borges Thompson
Thomas Milton Kemnitz

Royal Fireworks Press
Unionville, New York

UNION (CWA) LABEL
PRINTING SECTOR
UNIONVILLE, NY
ROYAL FIREWORKS PRESS 22

Drawing by Milton Kemnitz

Royal Fireworks Publishing Company
First Avenue, P.O. Box 399, Unionville, NY 10988
845 726-4444   FAX 845 726-3824
Email: mail@rfwp.com
ISBN: 978-089824-464-9 Student Book
978-089824-466-3 Teacher Manual
Printed in the United States of America
on acid-free paper using vegetable-based inks
by the Royal Fireworks Printing Company
of Unionville, New York.

Design by Michael Clay Thompson
All photos by Dr. Thomas Milton Kemnitz
Drawing by Milton Kemnitz

Table of Contents

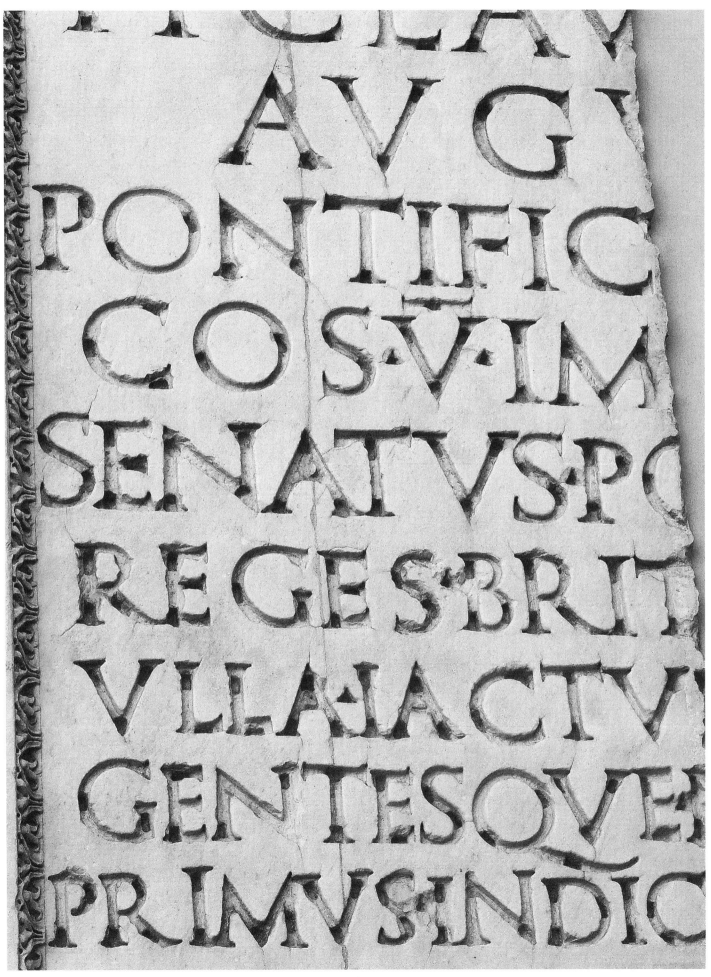

FOREWORD
FOR STUDENTS

Get ready for some serious fun. This classical education edition of *Caesar's English* has been designed especially for you. We have spared no effort to make this book an amazing experience. It is filled with photos, maps, facts, ideas, grammar, poems, writing challenges, and words that will give you a deep look at ancient Roman civilization and the effect of that civilization on the modern English language. Without realizing it, we speak Latin, or slightly altered Latin, much of the time. Thousands of English words are still spelled the same way and still mean the same thing that they did during the Roman empire, two thousand years ago.

Unlike Spanish or other Romance (descended from Roman Latin) languages, English does not descend directly from Latin, the language that the Romans spoke. English is a Germanic language, but during the sixteen centuries since Rome fell, English has acquired thousands of Latin-based words—so many that words from Latin have come to dominate academic life in English. The further you progress in education, the more Latin-based words you encounter. English may not be a Romance language, but it feels like one, especially in higher academics.

For this reason, it is important to study the Latin prefixes, roots, and suffixes—we will call them *stems*—that combine to make the vocabularies of advanced academic subjects. The Latin stems make a kind of academic vocabulary construction set, and once you understand the set, you understand thousands of words easily—even words that you have never encountered before. Before you plunge into the book, let me give you some ideas that will help you get the most out of your work:

• Study the photos carefully. The photos have been selected from thousands taken by Dr. T.M. Kemnitz in Rome and elsewhere. The photos show important details about Roman life and architecture. You will see in the photos how massive, how truly enormous, Roman civilization was. One almost feels that these huge ruins must have been inhabited by a different species, twenty-feet tall. It is difficult to believe that such an impressive and powerful civilization could have fallen, but fall it did, and this is one of the extraordinary stories of world history.

• Explore the maps. In most cases, the maps are related to the texts on the facing pages. Use a globe in connection with your studies and get to know ancient Rome's part of the world. Learn not only the countries and land masses but the bodies of water as well.

• Focus on the important connection between Rome and Spain that has resulted in modern Spanish and that connects English and Spanish vocabulary today.

• Notice that many of the activities in the book are done with pencils down. Not every activity needs to involve writing. Some of the most important activities are careful reading, thinking, rereading, rethinking, and discussing. You will see that there is an emphasis on reading and on big ideas, rather than on memorizing trivial facts.

• Remember that vocabulary is not a separate subject, apart from grammar or writing. Every vocabulary word has a grammar function. It will be a noun, or an adjective, or a verb, or another part of speech, and it must be used in its grammatical way. All language skills are connected. Furthermore, every word has a past. Each word is a speck of history; it comes from Rome, or Greece, or the forests of Germany. Words are points of knowledge. Their regions of origin can often be found on a map.

• Soak up the sounds of words. One of the most important elements of vocabulary is sound. Words have special combinations of vowels and consonants, and these sounds, as the great British poet Shelley explained, have relationships to each other and to what they represent. We might choose scratchy or pounding or booming sounds to describe a storm, and soft, peaceful sounds to describe a gentle breeze. The more words you know, the more sound choices you have. That is why this book pays special respect to the poetic aspects of vocabulary.

• Look things up. This book is in part a preview, a set of hints, a maze of clues. We have filled the book with references to people, places, events, cities, wars, leaders, and other details that will make exciting research for you. Be enthusiastic about going beyond this book. Take charge. Use the book as a launching platform for your own, independent, self-directed learning.

We hope you enjoy this work as much as we have enjoyed creating it.

INTRODUCTION

Once upon a time...far, far away...

Long ago, far from our New World, a great civilization lived and died. Throughout the ancient world, they built roads, made laws, and wrote literature. Today, most of their buildings have crumbled to ruins, but echoes of their words still reverberate because the English language (and others, such as Spanish) is filled with fragments of their language, Latin.

The vanished civilization was Rome, in Italy, and Rome rose to power more than 2,000 years ago, which is more than twenty centuries.

Only 500 years ago, astonished Europeans discovered that there was an inhabited New World on the back side of the planet, and after three centuries of early conflict and exploration, a new nation—as Abraham Lincoln put it in his Gettysburg Address—was conceived on the North American continent.

In the 150 years since Lincoln spoke, this new nation—the United States—has conceived a new English, which is a combination of Roman Latin, ancient Greek, German Anglo-Saxon, Spanish, American Indian languages, and other tongues. Walt Whitman, the poet of *Leaves of Grass*, once wrote: "Thus far, impress'd by New England writers and schoolmasters, we tacitly abandon ourselves to the notion that the United States have been fashion'd from the British islands only, and essentially form a second England only—which is a very great mistake.... To that composite American identity of the future, Spanish character will supply some of the most needed parts."

Even with all of these influences, Latin, the language of ancient Rome, is still the most important source of academic English. The further you advance in education, the more Latin you encounter in English vocabulary. This is true even though the foundation of English is Germanic, and English is not, like Spanish or French, a Romance (descended from Rome) language. When it comes to academic English, the Latin frosting is larger than the German cake.

Latin Stems: In *Caesar's English* we will learn about our own language by learning about these Latin fragments hidden in it. Fragments? Yes. Many of our words are made of two or three fragments of Latin. We sometimes call these pieces *prefixes, suffixes, affixes, roots*, or *stems*, but to make our discussions simpler, we will usually call them *stems*.

You will find the stem *sub*, for example, in many English words. *Sub* usually means under, and we find *sub* in words such as *submarine, submerge*, and *subtract*. We also find *sub* in harder words, such as *subterranean, subordinate, substantial*, and even *subterfuge*.

Even though these Latin-based words seem hard at first, the truth is that they are not as hard as they look—if you know the Latin stems. The word *subterranean*, for example, is only a combination of *sub*, under, and *terr*, land. A cave is subterranean because it is under land. Most big words or hard words are not difficult if you know the Latin stems that are in them.

Each time you learn one important stem, you have learned a part of dozens of English words; so learning Latin stems is power-learning because you only have to study one small thing in order to learn dozens of things.

In this book you are going to learn many Latin stems. As you learn more and more, you will begin to notice them everywhere. You will find Latin stems in the words of newspapers, books, and news programs. You will hear educated adults use words that have Latin stems. You will sometimes hear a word for the very first time, but you will know what it means anyway because you know the Latin stems in it.

You now see why this book is the preparation for a vocabulary textbook series called *The Word Within the Word*—because our modern English words have these ancient Latin fragments inside them. There are ancient words inside our modern words, and we are going to find out what they are.

Classic Words: A second feature of this book is a series of words that are prominent in the classic books of American and British literature. These classic words are almost all of Latin origin (there are some from other sources), which is yet another indication of the powerful importance of Latin to modern English. In lessons that feature these great Latin-based words, you will see that they have been used by famous writers of English literature for centuries and have formed a central core of advanced literary language. The words you will learn are so central that you will find them in almost every good book you ever read.

The definitions you will learn of these classic English words are only a beginning. When you learn the word *exquisite* and the definition we use here (beautifully made), you must realize that, like most words, *exquisite* has other related meanings; it can also mean intricate, delicate, flawless, and other similar things. Think flexibly.

The quizzes in this book are cumulative. In other words, the quiz on Lesson IV is really on Lessons I through IV. You must be a proud, disciplined student, reviewing all lists for all quizzes. Think in terms of permanence; the goal is to learn these stems and words now and to know them for the rest of your life. That is important because they are of such high quality that you will always need them.

We have taken pains in this book to frame our vocabulary study in the light of a vanished Roman culture. You will see images from Rome, read quotations from Roman philosophers, and learn Roman facts. Remember that this is not just imaginary; the language you speak and think is a collection of echoes from the ancient past—from Julius Caesar's world.

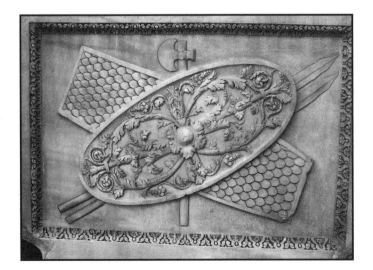

DIVIDE ET IMPERA.

Divide and conquer.

- Julius Caesar

LATIN STEMS · LESSON I

stem	meaning	modern examples
bi	two	bicycle, biped, bilateral
sub	under	submarine, submerge, subtract
de	down	descend, deposit, deduce
pre	before	predict, prepare, prelude
super	over	supervise, superior, superb

BI means two. A *bicycle* has two wheels. A biped (like you) has two feet. *Bilateral* means two-sided, and a *bimonthly* magazine comes out every two months.

SUB means under. A *submarine* goes under the sea. To *submerge* is to pull something under the surface, and to *subtract* is arithmetic in which you take away (*tract* - pull, *sub* - under) one number from another.

DE means down. To *descend* is to go down. To *deposit* is to put down. To *deduce* is to think your way down from a big truth.

PRE means before. To *predict* is to announce something before it happens. To *prepare* is to get ready before an event. A *preschool* is an early school before first grade, and a *prelude* is the music before a performance.

SUPER means over. To *supervise* is to watch over people. A *superman* is someone with powers over and above the norm. *Superior* means over others in quality and so does *superb*. Notice that *super* and *sub* are opposites.

view preexist prefect preheat precede
season preliminary precinct prefigure
prefix preorder prefabricate precursor
judge preliterate prearrange preclude
id precocious premolar premeditated
quisite prepare presocratic prejudice
ained prepare preoccupy prenominal
minate predispose preexist preocular
precognition prefer preface predorsal
classical prefab precondition prelate
wn precalculus precinct predilection
rate precipitate premise precognition
storic prenatal preconfigure prejudge
ool precedent preordained preamble
ink premonition preexist predecessor
ed pretend prefer preface precolonial
rding prehensile precession prefigure
ition preeminent predestined predate
pitate premise precambrian prebiotic
al prelude prejudge pretrial prejudice
ined preamble precession predispose

NONFICTION WORDS

Here are five important nonfiction words. You will not hear them in daily conversation, but you will encounter them frequently in your future academic life.

stem	word	definition
bi	**bicameral**	having two chambers
sub	*sub rosa*	done in secret
de	**debrief**	to question someone
pre	**preexist**	existing beforehand
super	**superannuated**	obsolete

BICAMERAL is an adjective that refers to a legislative body, such as a bicameral Congress that has two chambers. One example is the U.S. House of Representatives and Senate.

SUB ROSA is usually used as an adjective and means done in secret. The rose was a traditional symbol of secrecy. Example: The two spies conducted a *sub rosa* conversation. We italicize *sub rosa* because it is in a foreign language, in this case Latin.

DEBRIEF is a verb that describes a formal questioning process such as the government might conduct after an agent returns from an important mission.

PREEXIST is a verb, but we also often see it as the adjective *preexisting*. We could say that American Indians preexisted the Europeans on the North American continent, or we could say that someone could not attend because she had a preexisting obligation.

SUPERANNUATED is an adjective that means obsolete or out of date. Someone might have a superannuated computer.

Write two good sentences for each word.

CAESAR'S ANALOGIES

Many important tests that you take in the future will have analogies in them. An analogy is a logic challenge in which two relationships resemble each other. For example, *a giant is tall* as *a mountain is high*. In each case the adjective describes the height of the noun; it is a characteristic of the vertical dimension of the noun. We express an analogy this way:

PRELUDE : POSTLUDE ::
   a. tire : car
   b. window : house
   c. prologue : epilogue
   d. red : sunset

The answer:

PRELUDE : POSTLUDE :: PROLOGUE : EPILOGUE
PRELUDE **is to** POSTLUDE **as** PROLOGUE **is to** EPILOGUE.

In this arrangement, one colon means *is to*, and a double colon means *as*. We would say, "Prelude *is to* postlude *as* prologue *is to* epilogue." Notice that only one of the four answers is best: prologue/epilogue. A prologue is a section at the beginning of a book, and an epilogue is a section at the end of a book. Red is not before the sunset; it is the color of it. Tire does not come before a car; it is a part of it.

Sometimes a relationship is like *green* and *leaf*; one word is a characteristic of the other. Sometimes the relationship is of opposites:

up is to *down* as *full* is to *empty*. Sometimes the relationship is of part and whole: *dial* is to *radio* as *handle* is to *drawer*. Sometimes the relationship is of synonyms: *dark* is to *obscure* as *bright* is to *luminous*. There are many different kinds of relationships, but we are looking for two terms that have the same relationship to each other that the first pair has.

Sometimes it helps to put the relationship into a sentence so that you can clarify the meaning. For example, for the terms *student* and *class*, you might say, "The student is a member of the class." That way, if you saw the terms *musician* and *band*, you could say, "The musician is a member of the band."

It is important to realize that the relationship in the second pair must be in the same direction as the relationship in the first pair. For example, if we use the part-to-whole relationship, we might have *chimney is a part of a house as fender is a part of a car*. So *chimney : house :: fender : car* works. But if it were switched to *chimney : house :: car : fender*, it would be false. See if you can solve the following analogy:

        DESCEND : ASCEND ::
           a. bicycle : tricycle
           b. submerge : emerge
           c. man : superman
           d. school : preschool

Caesar's Spanish

stem	meaning	English / Spanish
bi	*two*	bicycle / bicicleta
sub	*around*	submarine / submarino
de	*down*	deposit / depositar
pre	*before*	predict / predecir
super	*over*	superlative / superlativo

Look closely at each pair of cognates (words that are relatives), and notice that English and Spanish both contain fragments from ancient Roman Latin. Unlike Spanish, which is a Romance language, English has a Germanic, Anglo-Saxon basis, but it has received thousands of Latin elements during the centuries. These Latin-based words now comprise the core of our academic vocabulary, and there are thousands of English-Spanish cognates that are nearly identical, containing one or more of the same stems.

A Roman Fact

When the Roman Emperor Vespasian was shown a hoisting machine that would reduce the need for workmen in construction, he refused to use the machine. He explained, "I must feed my poor."

CAESAR'S WORD SEARCH

In the puzzle, find the Latin-based English words that you see below. They might be vertical, horizontal, or diagonal. Always notice the stems that are in the words.

```
T P A I T M U V A E A D E P I B
P I E C C N M S U C D C P P P N
R G S G A D E S C E N D M G V C
U O U U R A S U B M A R I N E R
I I P E T M O E A E N I R V U B
G M E M B B Y S Y R E B U D S Y
T D R M U I B I N A A I I A Y S
I I I E S C O V A A M L B I U E
S B O D I Y D R A M T A Y B Y P
O P R U V C E E D S U T M P U R
P P M L R L D P R E O E P V Y E
E G S E M E U U G Y R R R V P P
D B P R E G C S T G T A A V V A
M I S P G R E I E V E L L V L R
B R E P U S D Y O N C B L M O E
M U T C I D E R P O A M M P A M
```

bicycle	bilateral	biped	deduce
deposit	descend	predict	prelude
prepare	submarine	submerge	subtract
superb	superior	supervise	

1. Which of these fifteen words is the most interesting?
2. Which of these words will you use most often?
3. Which two words are related to each other in some way?
4. Which word sounds most scholarly or academic?
5. Which word has the most precise meaning?

CAESAR'S GRAMMAR · PARTS OF SPEECH

We must use vocabulary correctly, and it is grammar that provides the instructions for correct vocabulary usage. Therefore, in *Caesar's English* we discuss usage in terms of *parts of speech*, which is the first of four levels of grammar. The parts of speech are the eight kinds of words in English. There are two main parts of speech—noun and verb—and six lesser kinds words that work with them. The abbreviations of the parts of speech are noun (n.), pronoun (pron.), adjective (adj.), verb (v.), adverb (adv.), preposition (prep.), conjunction (conj.), and interjection (interj.).

NOUN - names a person, place or thing
PRONOUN - takes the place of a noun
ADJECTIVE - modifies a noun or a pronoun

VERB - shows action, being, or links a subject to another word
ADVERB - modifies a verb, adjective, or another adverb

PREPOSITION - shows a relationship between things
CONJUNCTION - joins two words or two groups of words
INTERJECTION - shows emotion

Yes,	he	suddenly	saw	the	tall	Roman	and	the	short	Gaul.
interj.	pron.	adv.	v.	adj.	adj.	n.	conj.	adj.	adj.	n.

Every word is one of these eight kinds. We will explore this first level of grammar for five lessons. When we get to Lesson VI, we will add a second level of grammar, a third level at Lesson XI and a fourth at Lesson XVI. You can find a full exploration of grammar in *Grammar Town*.

1. Caesar watched the Gauls and **deduced** their strategy.
   n.   v.   adj.   n.   conj.   v.   adj.   n.

2. The noisy charge was only a **prelude** to the main attack.
   adj. adj. n. v. adv. adj. n. prep. adj. adj. n.

3. The creature was a **biped** and walked on two feet.
   adj. n. v. adj. n. conj. v. prep. adj. n.

4. The veteran ninth legion had a **superb** sense of discipline.
   adj. adj. adj. n. v. adj. adj. n. prep. n.

5. A grizzled old prophet **predicted** the defeat of the army.
   adj. adj. adj. n. v. adj. n. prep. adj. n.

Study these five sentences carefully. *Deduced* is a verb because it is an action that Caesar is taking. *Prelude* is a noun; it is the name of a situation, and it is modified by the adjective *a*. *Biped* is also a noun, modified by an adjective; in this case *biped* is the name of a creature. *Superb* is an adjective that modifies the noun *sense*. Finally, *predicted* is a verb that shows the action of the noun *prophet*.

Look closely the adjectives in the five sentences. Do you see how every adjective is paired with the noun it modifies? We see *the/Gauls*, *their/strategy*, *noisy/charge*, *main/attack*, *two/feet*, *ninth/legion*, *old/prophet*.

In addition to these adjectives, we see a special kind of adjective called the *article*; the articles are the three adjectives *a*, *an*, and *the*. We know that they are called *articles*, but we will usually refer to them simply as *adjectives* because that is their primary job—to modify nouns. Sometimes people call them *article adjectives*, but we will not do that because it is not standard terminology. The articles are adjectives.

476 A.D.

Michael Clay Thompson

No Roman sage predicted this.
These ruins, deposited, that fifteen
centuries of constant time have cracked.
Superb Corinthian columns stacked, now
fractured stones upon the grass, that once upheld
the roofs, the proofs of power evicted, felled,
descended now, this hour, brought low.

Now tourists tread their biped paths,
deducing from the fallen columns
all in line, subtracting time. A child
bicycles through the ruins, laughs, a prelude
to the afternoon, the heat, the photographs,
deductions of some wild destruction past.

Barbarian hordes invaded here, crashed in,
the Visigoths, Caesar long gone by then.
Rome's preparation lacked precision, slacked,
and roughneck brutes destroyed the place.
No supervision—swords and screams and wrath,
and then the late superior empire
crumbled blasted, the city's great interior streets
submerged beneath the roaring horde.

476 A.D.

Translated by Myriam Borges Thompson

Ningún sacerdote romano lo predijo.
Estas ruinas, **depositadas**, hace quince siglos,
del paso constante del tiempo, se han craqueado.
Columnas corintias **soberbias**, ordenadas,
ahora pedazos de piedras entre la hierba, que una vez
soportaron los techos, las evidencias del triunfo, cayeron,
descendieron ahora, a esta hora, hasta lo profundo.

Ahora, los turistas se desplazan **bípedos** por los senderos
deduciendo de las columnas caídas,
alineadas, **substrayendo** el paso del tiempo. Un niño
en **bicicleta** atraviesa las ruinas, se ríe, un **preludio**
de la tarde, del calor, las fotografías,
las **deducciones** de alguna pasada **destrucción** salvaje.

Tribus de bárbaros invadieron aquí, chocaron,
los visigodos, ya desaparecido César para aquel entonces.
La **preparación** carecía de **precisión**,
rufianes y brutos **destruyeron** aquel lugar.
Sin **supervisión**, pero con espadas, gritos y rabia,
así un imperio **superior** de la antiguedad,
derribado, las grandes calles intramurales
sumergidas en el alarido de la manada.

JULIUS CAESAR, PART I

When Gaius Julius Caesar was born in July of 100 B.C.—probably in Rome—no one could have predicted that he would become one of the colossal figures of world history, a superb military genius and the author of one of the most profound texts of the ancient world, the *Commentaries on the Gallic War*.

Caesar was descended from a patrician (noble) Roman family. His father was also named Gaius Julius Caesar, and his mother was Aurelia Cotta. When Caesar was only sixteen years old, his father died, leaving him to supervise the family. Only one year later, Caesar was nominated to be the high priest of Jupiter, but to qualify, he had to be married to a patrician, and so he ended his preexisting engagement to a plebeian (non-noble) girl and married Cornelia, the daughter of the patrician Lucius Cinna.

Lucius Cornelius Sulla, then the emperor-dictator of Rome, decided to rid Rome of his political enemies, and he began to have them exiled or even killed. Because Caesar was married to Cinna's daughter, Sulla deduced that Caesar was his enemy and stripped him of his fortune and priesthood. Caesar refused to divorce Cornelia, and he fled into hiding. Eventually, *sub rosa* political pressure caused Sulla to pardon Caesar, who was able to return to a position in Roman society.

As high priest of Jupiter, Caesar had been forbidden even to look upon an army. Now free of the duties of priesthood, he was able to pursue a military career. He left Rome, joined the Roman legions, and began the prelude to his life of military genius, a life in which he would shatter superannuated military traditions and develop superior, unprecedented strategies.

THE SEAS OF THE ROMAN EMPIRE

A: Pharsalus
B: Athens

IN HOC SIGNO VINCES.
In this sign shalt thou conquer.
- Constantine

CLASSIC WORDS · LESSON II

1. **countenance**: facial expression
2. **profound**: deep
3. **manifest**: obvious
4. **prodigious**: huge
5. **languor**: weakness

COUNTENANCE

The English noun *countenance* refers to the contents of the face. A person's countenance can be cheerful, stormy, or melancholy. You might see a smiling countenance or a morose (sad and gloomy) countenance. There could be a look of disappointment on the countenance. James M. Barrie wrote, in *Peter Pan*, that "This ill-luck had given a gentle melancholy to his countenance." In Robert Louis Stevenson's book *Dr. Jekyll and Mr. Hyde*, there is a man of "rugged countenance that was never lighted by a smile" and a "grave countenance." James Fennimore Cooper used *countenance* in his 1826 novel *The Last of the Mohicans*: "The countenance of Hawk-eye was haggard and careworn, and his air dejected."

Countenance is an old English word. Coming from the Latin *continentia*, it was even used by Geoffrey Chaucer in his 1385 poem *The Canterbury Tales*: "As I may best, I wol my wo endure, ne make no contenance of hevinesse." As you see, English spelling has changed in 600 years. It will change again in the coming centuries.

How would you describe the countenance of the Roman Emperor Constantine in the colossal statute on the facing page?

PROFOUND

The adjective *profound*, from the Latin *profundus*, means deep, and in a related way, it can also mean complete or even absolute. An ocean can be profound, but so can an idea, as in profound philosophy. There can be profound differences between people. Richard Wright wrote about a profound silence. In James M. Barrie's *Peter Pan*, Captain Hook was "profoundly dejected," which meant that he was deeply sad. Sylvia Plath described "the profound void of an empty stomach," and in *The Double Helix*, James Watson described "the heart of a profound insight into the nature of life itself." In *Why We Can't Wait*, Martin Luther King, Jr., wrote, "What silenced me was a profound sense of awe." In *Hamlet*, Shakespeare described Hamlet's odd behavior this way: "He raised a sigh so piteous and profound as it did seem to shatter all his bulk and end his being."

Could a countenance be profound?

What do you think Jonathan Swift meant in his 1726 book *Gulliver's Travels* when he described "profound learning"? In what way can learning be profound?

MANIFEST

The English adjective *manifest* comes from the Latin *manifestus* and means obvious. When something is manifest, it is completely apparent and open to view. The noun form of *manifest* is *manifestation*, and there is even a verb form: something can manifest itself, meaning make itself obvious or clear. In George Orwell's 1945 book *Animal Farm*, Orwell wrote that the pigs were "manifestly cleverer than the other animals." In his American philosophical classic *Walden*, Henry David Thoreau wrote that "the squirrels manifest no concern whether the woods will bear chestnuts this year or not." Martin Luther King, Jr., wrote that "The yearning for freedom eventually manifests itself."

Could confidence be manifest on your countenance?

What did Jack London mean when he wrote in *The Call of the Wild* that "To Buck's surprise these dogs manifested no jealousy toward him"?

PRODIGIOUS

The English adjective *prodigious*, from the Latin *prodigiosus*, means huge or marvelous. Things that are prodigious are amazing. Rachel Carson wrote in *Silent Spring* that in the wild, microscopic mites and other insects are present in "prodigious numbers." *Silent Spring* was a science book that helped warn the world of the dangers of DDT and other toxic pesticides. In *The Yearling*, Marjorie Kinnan Rawlings wrote that "The effort needed to move the dead weight was prodigious." In his play *The Crucible*, Arthur Miller wrote, "There is a prodigious stench in this place." Robert Louis Stevenson wrote about prodigious numbers of seagulls and of a "prodigious valley, strewn with rocks and where ran a foaming river."

Exactly what did Stevenson mean in *Treasure Island* when he wrote, "The Spaniards were so prodigiously afraid of him"?

LANGUOR

Languor is weakness, either of body or of mind. The noun *languor* comes from the Latin verb *languere*, to languish. If you are weak, weary, tired, or droopy, you are in a state of languor. The noun *languor* can transform and appear as the adjectives *languid* and *languorous* or as the verb *languish*. When we feel languor, our gestures and movements can be languid or languorous, such as the weak wave of the hand we make when we are tired. We can also speak in a tired, weak, languid way. The Irish writer James Joyce once wrote that "a languorous weariness passed over him." If it gets very hot, we might feel languid; in *The Secret Garden*, Frances Hodgson Burnett wrote, "In India she had always felt hot and too languid to care much about anything." In Grahame's *The Wind in the Willows*, the lazy Toad replies languidly. We can even describe things in nature this way: Joseph Conrad refers to the "oily and languid sea" in his novel *Heart of Darkness*. One of the best sentences comes from H.G. Wells, who described a Martian invasion in his novel *The War of the Worlds*. We never learn the name of the main character who narrates the book, but at one point he says, "My movements were languid, my plans of the vaguest."

Could it be manifest that you were profoundly languorous? Could you have a languid countenance?

WHO IS THAT WRITER?

James M. Barrie, the author of *Peter Pan*, was born in Kirriemuir, Scotland, in 1860. Barrie wrote plays and novels and viewed life as a great adventure. He wrote *Peter Pan* in 1904 when he was living in London. The classic story of Never Never Land stressed the theme of childlike innocence. Barrie died in 1937.

Marjorie Kinnan Rawlings, the author of *The Yearling*, was born in Washington, D.C. in 1896. She began writing when she was six years old and earned a degree in English from the University of Wisconsin. Rawlings fell in love with Florida during a visit to her brother-in-law in 1926 and returned in 1928 to buy seventy-two acres at Cross Creek near Gainesville. In 1939 *The Yearling* won the Pulitzer Prize. Rawlings died in 1953 at the age of fifty-seven.

CAESAR'S MATHEMATICS

Today we use Arabic numerals, such as *2*, *3*, or *6*, in our mathematics, but the ancient Romans used Roman numerals. This system did not contain a zero, and it used a combination of letters to represent numbers. The letters of the mathematical system were *I* for *one*, *V* for *five*, *X* for *ten*, *L* for *fifty*, *C* for *one hundred*, *D* for *five hundred*, and *M* for *one thousand*. In the Roman system, larger values usually come first; when a smaller value comes before a larger one, it is subtracted from the larger one, but when a smaller value comes after a larger one, it is added to it. Examples:

I - 1	II - 2	III - 3	IV - 4
V - 5	VI - 6	IX - 9	X - 10
XII - 12	XLIII - 43	LXI - 61	XC - 90
CXV - 115	DCII - 602	CM - 900	MMV - 2005

We often see Roman numerals used on modern buildings, in film credits, or in book covers to indicate dates. For example, the date 2006 would be represented as MMVI. The date 1947 would be:

MCMXLVII

M - 1,000, CM - 900, XL - 40, VII - 7

CAESAR'S WORD SEARCH

In the puzzle, find the Latin-based English words that you see below. They might be vertical, horizontal, or diagonal. Always notice the stems that are in the words.

```
N R E R R P R X D B S B B G E
L A D T F E S G A D U C E F I
A M R C D C N P T S P C X M I
N A L B M N R T S U E E P E R
G N L C T A M T U O R T M X E
U I L D S N P X O I A U R R C
O F D B U E U X U G N T B E U
R E N P B T S G L I N U I D D
C S U R N N U F F D U P C U E
R T O E R U B E R O A R A L D
G X F E O O T I E R T E M E U
D X O X S C R R P P E D E R F
E M R I A M A B U U D I R P O
U N P S G P C E S L O C A O N
F N C T N M T D O P I T L N F
```

countenance   languor   preexist   deduce

profound   bicameral   superannuated   prelude

manifest   *sub rosa*   superfluous   subtract

prodigious   debrief   predict

1. Which of these fifteen words has the most beautiful sound?
2. Which of these words will you see in novels?
3. Which word is most unusual?
4. Which word is the most scholarly or academic?
5. Which word has the most exact meaning?

CAESAR'S SPANISH

Everywhere we turn, language reveals to us that modern English and modern Spanish have remnants of ancient Latin:

Latin	Spanish	English
profundus	profundo	profound
manifestus	manifiesto	manifest
prodigiosus	prodigioso	prodigious
languidus	lánguido	languid

CAESAR'S SYNONYMS

Here are words that are similar to the words in our list, but are they exactly the same in meaning, or are they slightly different? For each word on our list, look up any synonym that you do not know; then pick one and explain the difference between it and our word.

countenance: visage, expression, physiognomy, look, aspect, presence, mien, air, lineament, appearance

profound: deep, far-reaching, absolute, thorough, penetrating, unqualified, enlightened, wise, sapient, sagacious, judicious

manifest: obvious, apparent, illustrate, evince, typify, embody, personify, distinct, conspicuous, evident, noticeable, observable, palpable, unmistakable, plain

prodigious: great, enormous, marvelous, extraordinary, large, powerful, vast

languor: dreaminess, laziness, listlessness, quiet, stillness, inertia, lassitude, inaction, idleness, dormancy, stupor, torpidity, sluggishness, stagnation, drowsiness, somnolence

CAESAR'S REWRITES

Here are sentences from famous books. In each case, rewrite the sentence into more ordinary words. Example from Marjorie Rawlings's *The Yearling*: "A languor crept over him." The rewrite: Little by little, he began to feel lazy.

From James Barrie's *Peter Pan*: "This ill-luck had given a gentle melancholy to his **countenance**."

From Jack London's *The Call of the Wild*: "To Buck's surprise these dogs **manifested** no jealousy toward him."

From Frances Hodgson Burnett's *The Secret Garden*: "In India she had always felt hot and too **languid** to care much about anything."

From Mark Twain's *Tom Sawyer*: "The middle-aged man turned out to be a **prodigious** personage—no less than the county judge."

From Ralph Ellison's *Invisible Man*: "I felt **profoundly** sad, as though winter had fallen during the hour."

prodigious

Caesar's Antonyms

For each of the words in this lesson, think of a word that means the opposite, known as an *antonym*.

1. **countenance**
2. **profound**
3. **manifest**
4. **prodigious**
5. **languor**

Are there any words in this list that have no antonyms? Are there any for which it is difficult to think of an antonym? Why?

Caesar's Analogies

Analogies are about relationships. Find a second pair of words that have the same relationship to each other as the first pair has. Remember that it sometimes helps to put the two words into a sentence that makes the relationship clear.

MANIFEST : OBSERVABLE ::

    a. acute : pain

    b. odious : lovable

    c. languor : weakness

    d. condescend : admire

WISDOM : PROFOUND ::

    a. acute : blunt

    b. prodigious : microscopic

    c. countenance : expression

    d. languor : weak

SONNET FOR CONSTANTINE

Michael Clay Thompson

A countenance imperial, a face
prodigious, manifesting confidence.
A gaze profound, surveying empty space.
The sneer of cold command* is evident.

No whispers, no *sub rosa* hints from him,
no languor, no obsequious courtesy.
No hesitation, no prelude, no whim;
a preexisting air of certainty.

A prisoner debriefed, a truth deduced,
a fact subtracted from a German's tale:
attacks predicted on Byzantium—news—
old walls repaired against ballistic hail.

The capital of Constantine—superfluous?—
Constantinople on the Bosporus.

*An allusion to Percy Shelley's poem "Ozymandias." This poem thus compares Constantine's power to the power of the Egyptian pharaohs. This poem is an English sonnet: four quatrains and a couplet in iambic pentameter, rhyme scheme abab cdcd efef gg. The three blank lines that separate the quatrains and couplet are not typically present. For more information on the elements and rules of poetry, see *Building Poems*. *Obsequious* is an adjective that means groveling or repulsively subservient.

SONeto para Constantino

Translated by Myriam Borges Thompson

Un **continente** imperial, una faz
prodigiosa, **manifiesta** confianza.
Una mirada **profunda**, mide el vacío espacio.
El desprecio del frío mandato es **evidente**.

Sin susurros, ni sugerencias *sub rosa*
ni **languidez**, o cortesía obsequiosa.
Sin hesitación, **preludio**, o capricho;
un aire **preexistente** de certeza.

Un prisionero interrogado, una verdad **deducida**,
un hecho **substraído** de su leyenda germana:
ataques **predichos** en Bizancio—nuevas—
viejas murallas reparadas contra la balística grana.

La capital de Constantino—¿algo **superfluo**?—
Constantinopla en el Bósforo.

JULIUS CAESAR, PART II

Some time after Caesar joined the army, Emperor Sulla died, and Caesar deduced that he could return to Rome. Sulla had confiscated Caesar's fortune, so Caesar purchased a small house in a humble section of Rome. He worked with the law and developed a powerful speaking style, a prelude to the oratory that would inspire his legions.

Caesar's confidence was manifest early in his career. When he sailed the Aegean Sea to study in Greece, Sicilian pirates kidnapped him. The pirates declared that they would ransom him for twenty talents of silver, but Caesar, with a serene countenance, demanded that they ask the prodigious sum of fifty talents and told them he would have them crucified. The languorous pirates regarded his threat as a joke. After his release, he assembled a fleet of ships, hunted the pirates down, and crucified them.

Caesar then returned to the army and fought with Roman legions in Asia to defeat an invasion. When he returned to Rome, he was elected military tribune, and then in 69 B.C., the year that his wife Cornelia died, he won a seat in the senate and was elected quaestor for Spain, which put him in charge of public revenue and expenditure. Serving in Spain, Caesar saw a statue of Alexander the Great, and with profound emotion he broke into tears as he realized what Alexander had already accomplished by his age.

When Caesar returned to Rome in 67 B.C., he married Pompeia, Sulla's granddaughter, and challenged two senators for election as Pontifex Maximus, the chief priest of Rome. Caesar was elected amid accusations of *sub rosa* bribery, and he divorced Pompeia after accusing her of scandalous behavior.

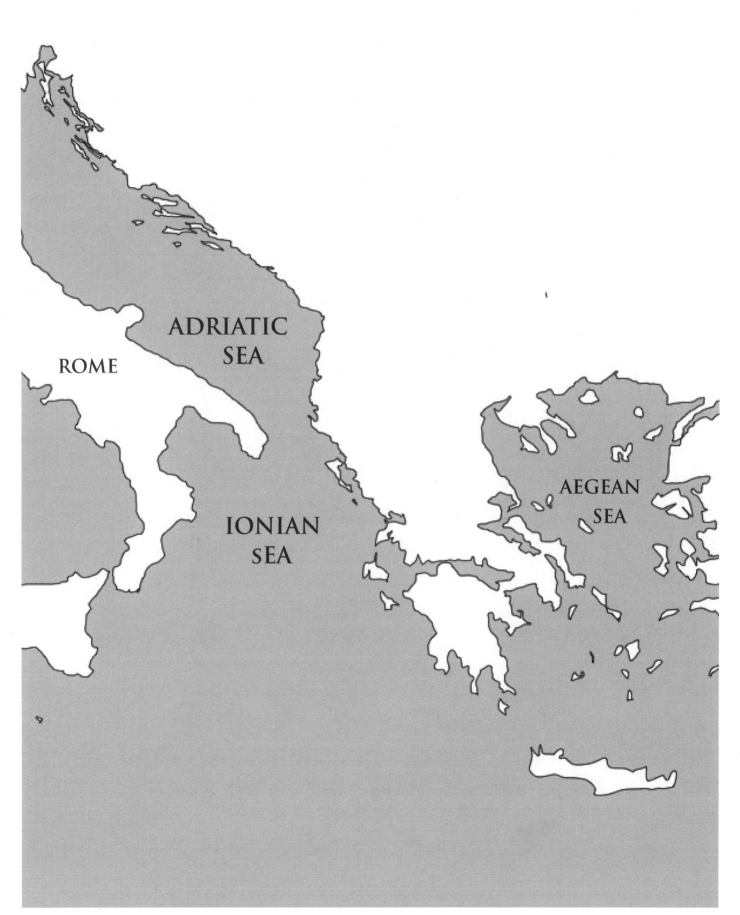

ROME

ADRIATIC
SEA

IONIAN
SEA

AEGEAN
SEA

CAESAR'S GRAMMAR · PARTS OF SPEECH

It is easy to forget that in some ways, vocabulary and grammar are the same subject. Every vocabulary word is a part of speech, and every sentence is made of vocabulary. To use vocabulary correctly, we must use it grammatically. Many words can be used in several ways. The word *run*, for example, can be a verb, as in *We run every day*; it also can be a noun: *We had a good run*.

Carefully study the grammar of our vocabulary below. On the line below each sentence, write the part of speech of each word. If you have not already studied *Grammar Town* to master the eight parts of speech, then review the grammar summary in Lesson I before you try these sentences. Do not worry if it takes you a few lessons to catch on; you have time, and you will get used to these ideas soon. Notice common patterns such as adjective with noun, noun with verb, or preposition-adjective-noun.

1. His **countenance** had a fierce look, and the soldiers stared.

    _____

2. As they marched, the army sank into a weary **languor**.

    _____

3. A **prodigious** hunger put the legion in a bad mood.

    _____

4. A **manifest** anxiety spread through the outpost.

    _____

5. The treaty had a **profound** effect on the senators.

    _____

REVIEW FOR CUMULATIVE QUIZ II

bi	two
sub	under
de	down
pre	before
super	over

bicameral	having two chambers
sub rosa	done in secret
debrief	to question someone
preexist	existing beforehand
superannuated	obsolete
countenance	facial expression
profound	deep
manifest	obvious
prodigious	huge
languor	weakness

profound

CARTHAGO DELENDA EST.

Carthage must be destroyed.

- Cato the Elder

48

Latin Stems · Lesson III

stem	meaning	modern examples
un	not	undone, unable, unequal, unprepared
inter	between	interstellar, international, interject
semi	half	semicircle, semiformal, semiannual
dis	away	dismiss, distract, distort
sym	together	symphony, sympathy, symmetry

UN means not. An *undone* task is not completed. An *unprepared* person is not prepared. Being *unable* to do something means not being able to do it, and *unequal* ice cream cones are not equal.

INTER means between. In the universe, *interstellar* space is the space between the stars. An *international* agreement is an agreement between nations. An *interlude* is a break between two parts of a performance, and to *interject* your opinion into a conversation is to insert yourself between people who are trying to talk.

SEMI means half. A *semicircle* is a half circle. A *semiformal* event requires half-formal attire, and a *semiannual* event happens every six months—half a year.

DIS means away. To *dismiss* a class is to send the students away, and to *distract* someone is to draw his or her attention away.

SYM means together. In a *symphony* orchestra, musicians play together. When we have *sympathy* for someone, we have a feeling of togetherness with him or her. *Symmetry* is a togetherness in which each side has the same shape.

ercalate interleave interrupt interplay
gency interject interstate interchange
hase interferon interim interpretation
ergradation intercede interdependent
e intercolonial interface international
diction interdict intercessor interlace
tertidal intercom interrelate interfuse
nesh interfere intergrow intergalactic
interpellate interferometer interstate
nal intermix interhistoric intermezzo
um interconnect intercommunication
cine intermingle interstice interloper
ttent interrelate interdigitate interlard
se intersect intermediate intersession
ertwine interact interlude interdental
tary interlard intercalate intergalactic
city intercollegiate interline intercept
al interval internaut interfusion inter
euron interview intervene interrogate
ssor interagency interdenominational
al interlock intertextual intercultural

NONFICTION WORDS

Here are five important nonfiction words. You will not hear them in daily conversation, but you will encounter them in your future academic life. Each word is based on one of the stems in this lesson.

stem	word	definition
un	**unabashed**	not embarrassed
inter	**interdict**	a prohibition
semi	**semiannual**	twice a year or half-yearly
dis	**disarray**	disorganized or untidy
sym	**symbiotic**	mutually beneficial

UNABASHED is an adjective that means not embarrassed by what one has done, not ashamed. A guilty person might be unabashed, even when caught.

INTERDICT can be a noun or a verb, though the noun form is usually *interdiction*. In Emily Brontë's *Wuthering Heights*, a character "wept and writhed against the interdict...."

SEMIANNUAL is an adjective that means twice per year or for a half-year. Some magazines come out semiannually, and semiannual plants only live for half a year.

DISARRAY is usually a noun that describes a state of disorder, disorganization, or chaos. We say that plans were thrown into disarray by an unexpected event. An army can be thrown into disarray by an ambush.

SYMBIOTIC is an adjective that means mutually beneficial. Sometimes two creatures live together in a way that benefits them both, such as the clownfish and the sea anemone.

Caesar's Analogy

The first two words are related to each other in a special way. Is one before the other? Is one inside the other? Are they opposites? Find the pair below that has the same relationship as the first pair.

INTERSTELLAR : STARS ::
   a. semicircle : circle
   b. dismiss : convene
   c. air : marbles
   d. unequal: equal

Advanced Word: Symphonic

The adjective *symphonic* (simm-FONN-ik) contains the Latin stems *sym* (together) and *phon* (sound). *Symphonic* means harmonic, a condition in which sounds sound good—in harmony—together. *Symphonic* is an adjective; it can modify either a noun or a pronoun, so you could have symphonic music or even symphonic voices. Most big cities have a symphony orchestra, which plays symphonic music, which sounds symphonic to our ears.

Advanced Word: Interpose

The verb *interpose* is a good word. *Interpose* contains the Latin stems *inter*, between, and *pos*, put, and it means to put between, or to interject. People interpose their comments when they interrupt to say something, but we also can interpose an object between other things. For centuries, *interpose* has been used by great writers, including Milton, Swift, Austen, Cooper, Hawthorne, and Kipling. Jonathan Swift described the "interposition of a cloud" in *Gulliver's Travels*. In *The Last of the Mohicans*, James Fennimore Cooper wrote that it was "as if a supernatural agency had interposed in the behalf of Uncas." In his famous *Narrative*, Frederick Douglass wrote that "not one interposed a friendly word" and that "In this state I appeared before my master, humbly entreating him to interpose his authority for my protection." Emily Brontë, in her immortal novel *Wuthering Heights*, wrote that "She held her hand interposed between the furnace heat and her eyes." In *Kim*, Kipling wrote that "Father Victor saw Kim edging toward the door, and interposed a strong leg." In *A Passage to India*, E.M. Forster observed that "the chauffeur interposed aggressively." In 1895 Stephen Crane described a scene from the Civil War in his novel, *The Red Badge of Courage*: "A rolling gray cloud again interposed as the regiment doggedly replied," and in *The Lord of the Flies,* William Golding wrote that "the vivid phantoms of his day-dream still interposed between him and Piggy."

Which of these examples of *interpose* do you like the best?

How many different meanings of *interpose* do you see?

WHO IS THAT WRITER?

Emily Brontë, the author of the great romantic novel *Wuthering Heights*, was born in Thornton, Yorkshire, England, on July 30, 1818. She had one brother and three sisters, including Charlotte, who wrote the great novel *Jane Eyre*. Emily's mother died in 1824. Emily and her sister Charlotte wrote poems and novels when they were children, but when they published *Jane Eyre* and *Wuthering Heights* in 1847, their fame skyrocketed. Emily died in 1848, having caught a cold at her brother's funeral.

CAESAR'S SPANISH

Everywhere we turn, language reveals to us that modern English and modern Spanish are both descendants of ancient Latin:

stem	meaning	English / Spanish examples
un	not	unappealable / inapelable (un = in)
inter	between	international / internacional
semi	half	semicircle / semicírculo
dis	away	distract / distraer
sym	together	sympathy / simpatía

A ROMAN FACT

Roman Emperor Titus (pronounced TIE-tuss) was opposed to capital punishment. During his reign he executed no one and even had informers flogged. Once, two patricians (upper-class Romans) were caught in a plot to overthrow Titus, and rather than have them executed, Titus sent them a warning. Then, he sent a messenger to one of the conspirator's worried mothers, assuring her that he would not execute her son.

CAESAR's MATHEMATICS

For each number, give the Arabic form if it is Roman or give the Roman form if it is Arabic:

874 -   CMLXXI -
1152 -   MCCCVIII -
95 -   MCMXC -

CAESAR'S WORD SEARCH

In the puzzle, find the Latin-based English words.

```
D E H E H P M I F E I R B E D I
E T P G T T B I N T E R D I C T
H E D D Y S B I U E H G A A E Y
S D C P N S E S C M I M D N T N
A E S N R U Y F D A M Y D E B L
B T B E A O O M I I M O D O M A
A A O B M N D F B N S E M T B N
N U G M Y I E I O I A A R P Y G
U N P M A D A T G R O M R A F U
A N A R O S X N N I P T X R L O
L A I C E L O F N U O U I P A R
P R F F M E D R U U O U B C S Y
H E D U L X X O C T A C S O D S
H P R M T I Y I A B N L P D H I
E U O F D A M L S S U L R T H I
O S L O H S L G A T E S L T U A
```

languor	manifest	interdict	prodigious
debrief	profound	unabashed	countenance
sub rosa	preexist	bicameral	superannuated
disarray	symbiotic	semiannual	

1. Which of these fifteen words has the nicest sound?
2. Which of these words might you use in a science essay?
3. Which two words are most similar in some interesting way?
4. Which word will you use most often? Why?
5. Which word has the clearest meaning?

CAESAR'S GRAMMAR · PARTS OF SPEECH

Study the first four sentences, then identify the parts of speech of sentences five through eight.

1. Rome   had   a   **preexisting**   agreement   with   the   barbarian   tribe.
    n.   v.   adj.   adj.   n.   prep.   adj.   adj.   n.

    _____

2. The   Gauls   were   thrown   into   **disarray**   by   the   ambush.
    adj.   n.   v.   v.   prep.   n.   prep. adj.   n.

    _____

3. The   army   slowly   approached   the   **prodigious**   wall.
    adj.   n.   adv.   v.   adj.   adj.   n.

    _____

4. Before   the   battle   a   **profound**   silence   fell   upon   the   armies.
    prep.   adj.   n.   adj.   adj.   n.   v.   prep.   adj.   n.

    _____

5. Caesar   issued   an   **interdict**   against   riots   in   the   streets.

    _____

6. The Romans and the Gauls maintained   a   **symbiotic** relationship.

    _____

7. After   he   punished   the   pirates,   Caesar   was   **unabashed**.

    _____

8. The   Gauls   resumed   their   **semiannual**   invasions   of   Rome.

    _____

GIAN LORENZO BERNINI'S BUST OF MEDUSA

THE BALLAD* OF JUSTINIAN

Michael Clay Thompson

How unabashed his countenance,
How plain his interdict,
Barbarians in disarray,
Believing they've been tricked.

No symbiotic truce for Jus',
No semiannual peace,
No words profound dilute the acts,
No languor at his ease.

Justinian rewrote the code,
With justice manifest.
The superannuated mode,
Replaced by stricter tests.

*A ballad stanza is a four-line poetic stanza, a quatrain, in which lines one and three are iambic tetrameter, and lines two and four are iambic trimeter. Because in a traditional ballad stanza lines one and three do not rhyme, but lines two and four do rhyme, the stanza reaches perfection in the final syllable of the stanza. Robert Burns and Emily Dickinson were masters of the ballad stanza.

CAESAR'S PARAGRAPH

We study the language arts—grammar, vocabulary, poetry, writing—as though they were different subjects, but in real sentences all of the elements come together. Vocabulary is the raw material for sentences. The writing textbook for this level of our curriculum is *Paragraph Town*, a deep exploration of the elements of a well-written paragraph.

The essence of any good paragraph is unity: every sentence in a paragraph is about the same topic, and the sentences are intelligently organized. The sentences might be organized from close to far, from then to now, from east to west, from not understanding to understanding, or from happy to sad. A paragraph, for example, might begin with a sentence about the closest thing, then something farther away, and then something in the distance.

Using words and stems we have studied, write a well-organized paragraph that contains at least five sentences. The paragraph should have something to do with ancient Rome, so you may need to do some reading in order to choose something interesting to write about. Try to work our vocabulary into the sentences in a natural-sounding way, and use correct grammar for the vocabulary.

This should be academic writing—school writing—which means that you should not use first person (*I, me*), and you are not allowed to use contractions (*isn't, didn't, don't*).

JULIUS CAESAR, PART III

During his governorship of Spain, Caesar conquered two tribes and reformed the debt laws, and he was admired for his effective leadership. Proud in countenance, he was entitled to return to Rome to receive a triumph, a public festival in his honor, but in 59 B.C. he wished to run for consul, which was the most powerful office in the Roman republic, and an interdict prohibited military commanders from running for consul. To run, Caesar had to resign his command of the army.

In an election tinged with disarray and scandal, Caesar won, though he had to receive financial support from two men who were enemies of each other—Crassus and Pompey. Caesar was able to craft a symbiotic alliance with the two men, and the three together were known as the First Triumvirate. This alliance was made stronger by Pompey's marriage to Caesar's daughter Julia. Caesar had divorced his second wife Pompeia, and now, unabashed, he married Calpurnia, the daughter of a Roman senator.

As consul Caesar made a prodigious decision—to distribute public lands to the poor. The idea had manifest support from both Crassus and Pompey, and they ordered soldiers into Rome to enforce the policy. One profound opponent of the law, Bibulus, tried to avoid the land distribution with a superannuated method—by claiming the omens were unfavorable, but Caesar's forces drove Bibulus from the forum. To avoid violence, Bibulus retreated to his home for a year and issued *sub rosa* communications.

After considerable maneuvering, Caesar was appointed to govern Cisalpine Gaul, Illyricum, and Transalpine Gaul and was given command of four legions for a term of five years. The matter settled, Caesar departed in haste for his new military duties.

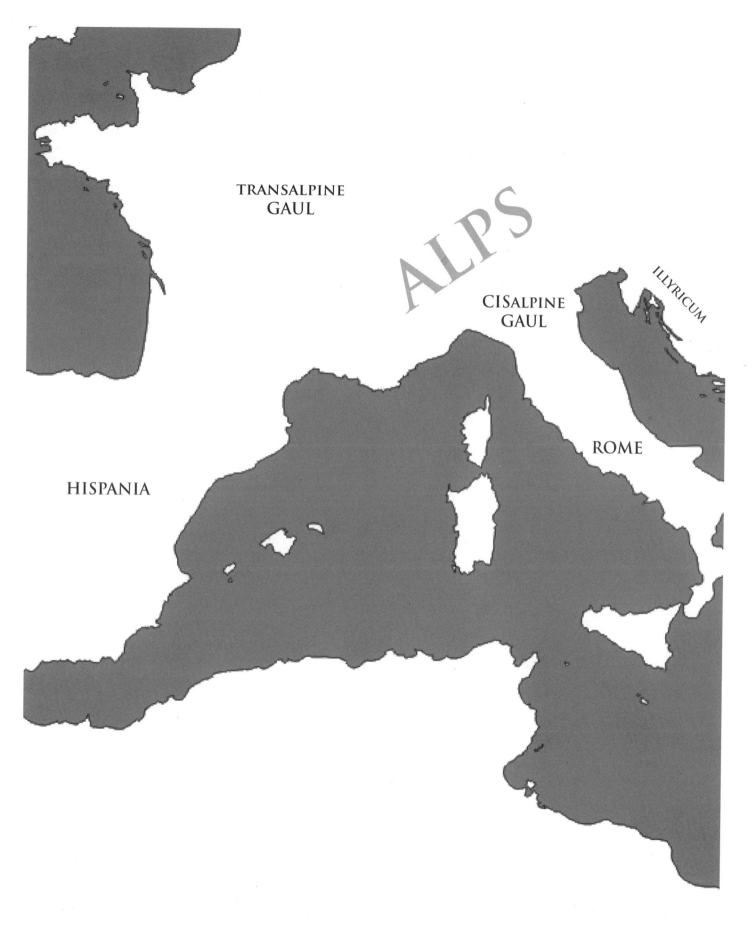

TRANSALPINE
GAUL

ALPS

CISALPINE
GAUL

ILLYRICUM

ROME

HISPANIA

TRANS - ACROSS
CIS - ON THIS SIDE OF

Review for Cumulative Quiz III

bi	two
sub	under
de	down
pre	before
super	over
un	not
inter	between
semi	half
dis	away
sym	together

bicameral	having two chambers
sub rosa	done in secret
debrief	to question someone
preexist	existing beforehand
superannuated	obsolete
countenance	facial expression
profound	deep
manifest	obvious
prodigious	huge
languor	weakness
unabashed	not embarrassed
interdict	a prohibition
semiannual	twice a year or half-yearly
disarray	disorganized or untidy
symbiotic	mutually beneficial

ROMAN LEGIONS HAD UP TO 5,000 SOLDIERS, OFTEN FEWER. THIS
DIAGRAM DEPICTS TWO LEGIONS.

CLASSIC WORDS · LESSON IV

1. **serene**: calm
2. **acute**: sharp
3. **grotesque**: distorted
4. **condescend**: to patronize
5. **odious**: hateful

SERENE

The adjective *serene* means calm, clear, peaceful. *Serene* comes to English from the Latin *serenus*, which came to Latin from the ancient Greek *xeros*, which meant dry. When a sky is dry, it has no clouds, rain, or storms in it; it is clear and peaceful. Kenneth Grahame, in *The Wind in the Willows*, described "the moon, serene and detached in a cloudless sky." A person's face can be like a peaceful, cloudless sky, too, as when Thomas Hardy wrote of his character's "serene Minerva-eyes" in *The Mayor of Casterbridge*. When we are deeply at peace in our hearts, this internal calm can be called *serene*; Henry David Thoreau, the American thinker who wrote *Walden* about his experiences in the woods, said that "my serenity is rippled but not ruffled." Mary Shelley used *serene* in her novel *Frankenstein*: "A serene sky and verdant fields filled me with ecstasy." Curiously, Shelley also described "serene joy," although the two words seem to suggest very different things. In Jane Austen's novel *Pride and Prejudice*, we read about "the serenity of your sister's countenance."

What would a serene countenance look like? How would it be like a serene sky, or a serene sea?

ACUTE

The English adjective *acute*, meaning sharp, can be traced back to the ancient Romans, where *acus* meant needle in Latin. In mathematics an acute angle is one that is fewer than 90 degrees. When someone has a sharp mind, we call that acute, too; in Jonathan Swift's story *Gulliver's Travels*, someone has a "most acute judgment." There is another sharp mind in Harriet Beecher Stowe's *Uncle Tom's Cabin*, where we see "an expression of great acuteness and shrewdness in his face." A sharp pain is acute; Jane Austen wrote that a character's "head ached acutely" in her novel *Pride and Prejudice*. In *The Yearling* Marjorie Rawlings wrote that "The gnawing in his stomach was an acute pain." Having a sense of justice is another kind of acute pain; in *Vanity Fair,* Thackeray asked, "who has a sense of wrong so acute, and so glowing a gratitude for kindness, as a generous boy?"

Do you think someone's mind could be both profound and acute? Could it be acute and serene at the same time?

GROTESQUE

The adjective *grotesque*, pronounced grow-TESK, comes to English from the Italian Renaissance, where workmen who were digging a foundation suddenly had the ground fall away from them, and a great hole opened up. When the workmen peered down into the opening, they could see that it was not a natural cavern; it was a ruin; they were staring down into ancient rooms. Soon they realized that they had discovered the long-buried remains of Roman Emperor Nero's great palace, which later emperors had destroyed. When the artist Raphael heard about the find, he raced across town and had himself lowered down into the hole on a rope. He carried a torch with him, and when he held out the torch, he could see strange, distorted artwork on the walls: weird animals and twisted human faces, creepy, exaggerated shapes. For the Italians this weird, distorted style became known by the underground grotto where it was found; it was *grotto-esque*, and our word *grotesque* is the result. Interestingly, the word *grotto* traces back to the vulgar Latin word *crypta*, hidden. We use the adjective *grotesque* to describe things that are physically weird-looking, such as in novelist John Gardner's *Grendel*, where he describes "grotesquely muscled shoulders." In *The Jungle,* Upton Sinclair wrote that a character "wore green spectacles, that gave him a grotesque appearance." H.G. Wells wrote in *The War of the Worlds* that "huge black shapes, grotesque and strange, moved busily to and fro." In Thornton Wilder's novel *The Bridge of San Luis Rey*, he wrote that the "almost grotesque and hungry face became beautiful." Joseph Conrad wrote that "they had faces like grotesque masks" in his novel *Heart of Darkness*.

We do not always, however, use *grotesque* to describe physical appearances. In *Tom Sawyer,* Mark Twain wrote that "He kept up this grotesque foolishness." In *Uncle Tom's Cabin*, Harriet Beecher Stowe described "one of those wild grotesque songs," and in *Grendel*, John Gardner wrote, "I scream, facing him, grotesquely shaking hands."

In what way is shaking hands grotesquely similar to grotesquely muscled shoulders? How are grotesque masks like grotesque foolishness? What are some other examples of grotesque things that you can think of?

CONDESCEND

To *condescend* usually means to act superior to someone else, to act as though you have to descend down to their inferior level, that is lower than your own. People who condescend might act as though it is unpleasant to converse with you, or as though they are doing you a favor to speak, and as though they are pleased with themselves for being so generous. In Harper Lee's novel *To Kill a Mockingbird*, Scout Finch says that her older brother "Jem condescended to take me to school the first day." In *Peter Pan*, Barrie wrote that "he would answer condescendingly." In Stephen Crane's masterpiece *The Red Badge of Courage*, about a young boy named Henry Fleming who goes to fight in the Civil War, Henry "reflected, with condescending pity: 'Too bad. Too bad. The poor devil, it makes him feel tough.'" In Emily Brontë's classic *Wuthering Heights*, "she was forced to condescend to our company." In Mark Twain's *Tom Sawyer*, "These two great commanders did not condescend to fight in person."

Sometimes *condescend* has a different meaning, one that is not so offensive to our feelings. It can refer to a situation in which someone in authority or high rank sincerely does something considerate for someone else, perhaps someone who is poor or helpless and who may appreciate the effort. In Charlotte Brontë's *Jane Eyre*, Jane says, "I did not feel insensible to his condescension, and would not seem so."

Interestingly, *condescend* is one of the oldest words in the English language. From the Latin *condescendere*, it was even used in 1385 by Geoffrey Chaucer in his poem *The Canterbury Tales* and in 1667 by Milton, who wrote in *Paradise Lost*, "Gentle to me and affable hath been / Thy condescension."

What do you think Thackeray meant in *Vanity Fair* when he wrote that "even great English lords and ladies condescended to speak to persons whom they did not know"?

Could someone condescend serenely? What would that mean?

ODIOUS

The adjective *odious*, from the Latin *odiosus*, refers to something that is repulsive, repugnant, hateful. We are disgusted by odious things that can be odious in appearance, in sentiment, or in many other ways. In Robert Louis Stevenson's *Dr. Jekyll and Mr. Hyde*, we read that "A flash of odious joy appeared upon the woman's face." Henry James gave the word a twist in his novel *The American*, writing, "You have been odiously successful." In *The House of the Seven Gables*, Nathaniel Hawthorne wrote, "Why do you keep that odious picture on the wall?" In Jane Austen's *Pride and Prejudice*, we read, "Pray do not talk to that odious man."

Could someone have an odious expression on his or her face? Is it odious to condescend? Could something be odious and grotesque at the same time? Could it be profoundly odious?

odious

WHO IS THAT WRITER?

Kenneth Grahame, the author of *The Wind in the Willows*, was born in Edinburgh, Scotland, in 1859. Grahame was educated at St. Edward's School, Oxford, and began professional life at the Bank of England. He began writing fiction in his spare time and originally wrote chapters of *The Wind in the Willows* as letters to his son, Alistair. Grahame died on July 6, 1932.

WHAT IS THIS WRITER SAYING?

Discuss the meanings of the **bold** words:

From Scott Fitzgerald's *The Great Gatsby*: "I see it as a night scene by El Greco: a hundred houses, at once conventional and **grotesque**, crouching under a sullen, overhanging sky and a lusterless moon."

From Mark Twain's *Tom Sawyer*: we "...heard the stony-hearted liar reel off his **serene** statement."

From Frances Hodgson Burnett's *The Secret Garden*: "The Rajah **condescended** to seat himself on a rug under a tree."

From Mark Twain's *Tom Sawyer*: "It made the going into captivity and fetters again so much more **odious**."

Caesar's Word Search

In the puzzle, find the Latin-based English words.

```
X T C I D E R P E D E D U C E S
S U B M R O S A N D O E F E C E
T T S E F I N A M Q U S M O G T
T S I X E E R P R S P L U X N U
S U O U L F R E P U S N E T E C
F T F O D I O U S P T P G R R A
X E M M P C U R R E D L L I P D
I S U P E R A N N U A T E D G E
X U I T U N X A N C A N F O B N
F B P L I E N E R E S O F B A M
E T L A C C B I C A M E R A L T
I R I N E P R O F O U N D G P L
R A C G A Q D N E C S E D N O C
B C P U A O O D L Q D Q L U U U
E T I O A U S U O I G I D O R P
D A D R C I E U Q S E T O R G R
```

countenance	languor	preexist	deduce
profound	bicameral	superannuated	prelude
manifest	*sub rosa*	superfluous	subtract
prodigious	debrief	predict	serene
acute	grotesque	condescend	odious

1. Which of these fifteen words is newest to you?
2. Which of these words do you like best?
3. Which of these words are nouns?
4. Which word is the most emotional?
5. Which word is the easiest to learn?

CAESAR'S GRAMMAR · PARTS OF SPEECH

Study the first four sentences, then identify the parts of speech of sentences five through eight.

1. His **odious** **countenance** frightened many Romans.
   adj. adj.   n.   v.   adj. n.

2. The emperor **condescended** and agreed to a meeting.
   adj. n.   v.   conj. v.   prep. adj. n.

3. A **serene** silence descended upon the camp as the sun set.
   adj. adj.   n.   v.   prep. adj. n. conj. adj. n. v.

4. A **grotesque** howl emerged from the barbarian army.
   adj. adj.   n.   v.   prep. adj. adj.   n.

5. Caesar had an **acute** genius for military strategy.

6. The **grotesque** appearance of the Gauls mattered little.

7. With **unabashed countenance**, the Gaul denied the crime.

8. The **semiannual** flood did not damage the city.

CAESAR'S ANTONYMS

For each of the words in this lesson, think of a word that means the opposite. A word that means the opposite is known as an *antonym*.

1. **serene**
2. **acute**
3. **grotesque**
4. **condescend**
5. **odious**

Are there any words in this list that have no antonyms? Are there any for which it is difficult to think of an antonym? Why?

CAESAR'S SYNONYMS

Here are words that are similar to the words in our list, but are they exactly the same in meaning? For each word on our list, look up any synonym that you do not know; then pick one and carefully explain the difference between it and our word.

serene: unclouded, bright, tranquil, placid, peaceful, quiet, still, unruffled, even, calm, asleep

acute: sharp, sensitive, perceptive, crucial, severe, intense, shrill, keen, penetrating, pointed, peaked, agonizing, fierce, knifelike, piercing

grotesque: distorted, ludicrous, macabre, incongruous, grisly, brutish, outlandish, monstrous, odious, nightmarish, ghastly, hideous, scary, bizarre, dreadful, shocking, fanciful

condescend: patronize, stoop, lower oneself, deign, descend

odious: hateful, abhorrent, repugnant, loathsome, detestable, disgusting, repulsive, appalling, deplorable, atrocious, abominable

CAESAR'S ANALOGIES

Analogies are about relationships. Find a second pair of words that have the same relationship to each other that the first pair has. Remember that it sometimes helps to put the two words into a sentence that makes the relationship clear.

SERENE : AGITATED ::

    a. loud : quiet

    b. profound : deep

    c. odious : mask

    d. countenance : strange

ACUTE : DULL ::

    a. sharp : knife

    b. odious : loveable

    c. serene : calm

    d. condescend : arrogant

CAESAR'S SPANISH

Everywhere we turn, language reveals to us that modern English and modern Spanish are both descendants of ancient Latin:

Latin	Spanish	English
acutus	agudo	acute
serenus	sereno	serene
condescendere	condescender	condescend
odiosus	odioso	odious

**GALLIA EST OMNIS
DIVISA IN PARTES TRES.**
All of Gaul is divided
into three parts.
- Julius Caesar

HADRIAN'S WALL

Michael Clay Thompson

Night watch. Odious post.
Acute cold from the north road
hacks its wrath. His face
cracks like the wall rocks.
Wall, wall, wall. Build the wall.
Guard the wall. Orders. Decius peers
over the wall at prodigious blacks
of hills in the dark. On some far
slope, he sees windblown sparks,
red tracks, the marks of fire. Enemy fire,
its guard staring back through the stark wind—
what else could it be? These preexisting Britons
are tough, not languorous savages in disarray
as his condescending commander joked.
They come from nowhere in grotesque forays,
sneak attacks, and vanish back, resisting,
into the profound, primeval black, a knack
for the serene danger of the unseen,
obscene enough to shock even a Roman.
Decius, unabashed about the fear-lash
that locks the back of his neck.
The fear is good. It is fear
that keeps him awake, listening
for the snapped twig.

CAESAR'S PARAGRAPH

There are different kinds of paragraphs. There are paragraphs for dialogue, for description, for the exposition of an argument or case, and for comparison, to name only a few.

Let us write a serious **descriptive** paragraph about Hadrian's Wall. Read about Hadrian's Wall and write a description of it, including good, factual details. Work in as many of this lesson's five words as you can, and add others from previous lessons. The paragraph can be long if you wish it to be. Remember to organize the sentences into a clear sequence so that they do not confuse the reader.

Remember that this is a vocabulary textbook, so the correct usage of the vocabulary words is the essence of this assignment. For example, the word *odious* is an adjective, so it must be used to modify a noun or pronoun. There might be an *odious howl*, or an *odious frown*, or an *odious act* of cruelty. By using our vocabulary in paragraphs, we learn two things at the same time: how to write a paragraph, and how to use our vocabulary correctly.

Once again this should be academic writing—school writing—which means that you should not use first person (*I, me*), and you are not allowed to use contractions (*isn't, didn't, don't*). In other words, never mention yourself, and always write with complete words. Just write about Hadrian's Wall. This should be academic in tone, so focus on facts; do not try to be cute or entertaining.

odious

CAESAR'S REWRITES

Here are some sentences from famous books. In each case, rewrite the sentence into more ordinary words.

From Jane Austen's *Pride and Prejudice*: "Her head ached **acutely**."

From Mary Shelley's *Frankenstein*: "He looks upon study as an **odious** fetter."

From Emily Brontë's *Wuthering Heights*: "She was forced to **condescend** to our company."

From H.G. Wells's *The War of the Worlds*: "The Martian, without using his Heat-Ray, walked **serenely** over their guns."

From Harriet Beecher Stowe's *Uncle Tom's Cabin*: "He could cut cunning little baskets out of cherry stones, could make **grotesque** faces on hickory nuts."

CAESAR'S MATHEMATICS

If CMLIII grotesque barbarians invaded Roman territory, and DCCXXXII retreated back into their own land, how many grotesque barbarians remained on Roman soil? Give the answer in Roman numerals.

JULIUS CAESAR, PART IV

When Caesar arrived in Gaul, the region was in disarray. Some tribes were in revolt; some were arming themselves to invade south toward Rome. Using his profound divide-and-conquer strategy, Caesar defeated the tribes one at a time. He also sent one legion to northern Gaul to prepare an invasion of Britain. In the spring of 56 B.C., Caesar met with the other two members of his Triumvirate, Crassus and Pompey, to strengthen their alliance.

In 55 B.C. two Germanic tribes ignored Rome's interdict and invaded northern Gaul, and Caesar drove them back, pushing his legions across the Rhine for manifest emphasis. He then turned his attention to Britain, but various odious conditions did not favor the invasion. Caesar tried again the next year, but after modest accomplishments he had to return to Gaul to quell new revolts.

When Caesar was in Britain, his daughter Julia, now Pompey's wife, died in childbirth. Pompey, unabashed, serenely married an enemy of Caesar's, and the Triumvirate collapsed.

In 52 B.C. a powerful revolt broke out in Gaul led by the charismatic Vercingetorix, a skilled military commander. After a number of engagements, Vercingetorix led his army to a fortified hilltop city, Alesia, thinking Caesar would go south for a languorous winter, but Caesar—no semiannual commander—followed Vercingetorix to Alesia, and laid siege to the city, building an enormous enclosing wall, a circumvallation, around Alesia. When prodigious Gallic armies came to rescue Alesia, Caesar acutely built a second set of walls outside the first, a double circumvallation, letting his legions fight in both directions, from inside the double walls. Eventually Vercingetorix surrendered and was carried as a prisoner back to Rome, where he suffered a grotesque end.

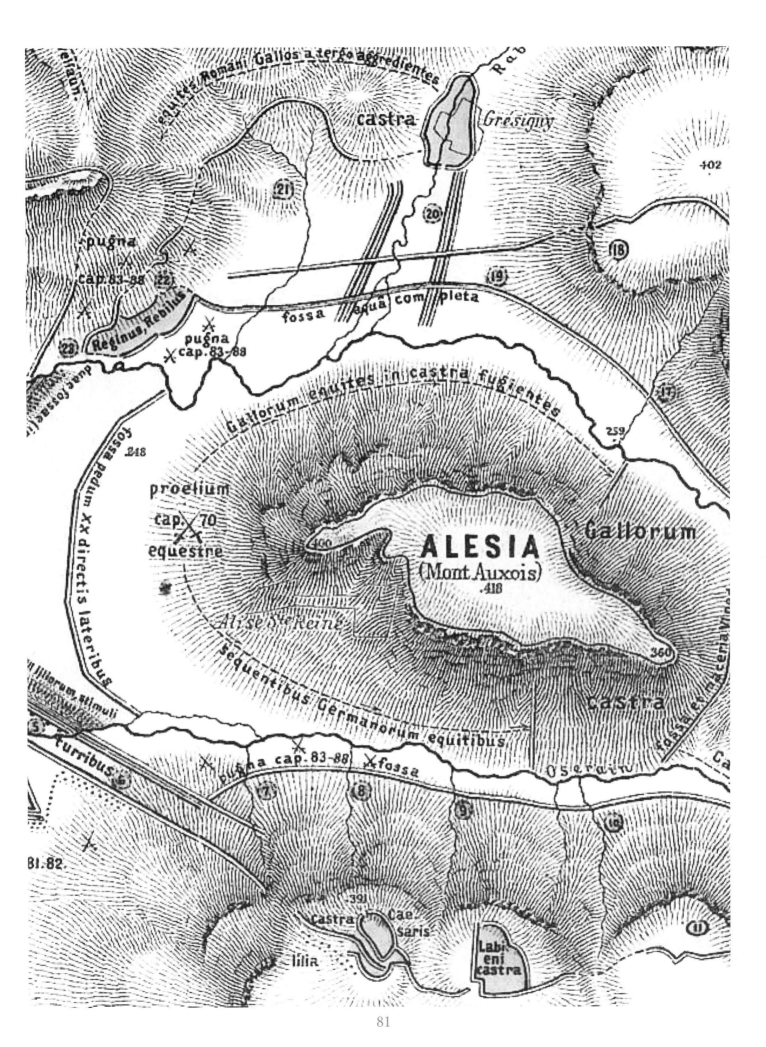

Review for Cumulative Quiz IV

bi	two
sub	under
de	down
pre	before
super	over
un	not
inter	between
semi	half
dis	away
sym	together
bicameral	having two chambers
sub rosa	done in secret
debrief	to question someone
preexist	existing beforehand
superannuated	obsolete
countenance	facial expression
profound	deep
manifest	obvious
prodigious	huge
languor	weakness
unabashed	not embarrassed
interdict	a prohibition
semiannual	twice a year or half-yearly
disarray	disorganized or untidy
symbiotic	mutually beneficial
serene	calm
acute	sharp
grotesque	distorted
condescend	to patronize
odious	hateful

CUM TACENT CLAMANT.
When they are silent, they cry out.
- Cicero

stem	meaning	modern examples
circum	around	circumnavigate, circumspect, circumvent
mal	bad	malevolent, malady, malicious
post	after	posthumous, postscript, posterity
equi	equal	equilateral, equivocate, equilibrium
ante	before	antebellum, antecedent, anterior

CIRCUM means around. A ship can *circumnavigate* the earth by sailing around it. To be *circumspect* is to be cautious and looking around, and to *circumvent* the rules is to get around them.

MAL means bad. A *malevolent* person has bad will or evil intentions. A *malady* is when you feel bad, and a *malicious* act is intentionally bad.

POST means after. A *posthumous* award is one given after its recipient has died. A *postscript* is the *PS* we put at the bottom of a letter after we have written it, and our *posterity* are our descendents who come after us.

EQUI means equal. An *equilateral* triangle has three equal sides, to *equivocate* is to take both sides of an issue equally, and *equlibrium* is a system in balance.

ANTE means before. The *antebellum* period is before the war. An *antecedent* is the noun that comes before its pronoun, and the *anterior* is the front part of something.

ostapproval postinvasion postlaunch
on postprison postcaucus postbellum
ostcolonial postmessianic postpartum
ude postorbital postmortem postcava
postdiluvian posthaste postindustrial
osthypnotic postglacial postprandial
surgical postern postdate postmodern
classical posterity postflight postdate
ssionism postvocalic postproduction
tnatal postgraduate postwar posterior
ostscript postdeployment postdecimal
ostcranial postcapillary postoperative
l postliterate postdoctoral postseason
ism posttest postposition postmodify
postlapsarian postfeudal postpartisan
ist postilion postmarket postgenomic
nillennial postdebate postpublication
tructural postassessment postnuclear
postliberation postinvasion postilion
numous postpatriarchal postmidnight
osthumous postprimary postfracture

NONFICTION WORDS

Here are five important nonfiction words. You will not hear them in daily conversation, but you will encounter them in your future academic life. Each word is based on one of the stems in this lesson.

stem	word	definition
circum	**circumvent**	get around
mal	**maladroit**	clumsy, bungling
post	**posterior**	at the back, later
equi	**equitable**	fair, impartial
ante	**anterior**	near the front, earlier

CIRCUMVENT is a verb that means to get around or overcome a problem in a crafty way. Sometimes people try to circumvent the rules.

MALADROIT is an adjective that means bungling or clumsy. Someone might offer a maladroit excuse for circumventing the rules.

POSTERIOR is an adjective or noun that refers to the back of something. There could be an injury to the posterior section of the brain.

EQUITABLE is an adjective that means fair or impartial. A leader could find an equitable solution to a dispute.

ANTERIOR is an adjective that refers to the front; it is the opposite of *posterior*. We might describe the anterior section of a building.

CAESAR'S ANALOGY

The first two words are related to each other in a special way. Is one before the other? Is one inside the other? Are they opposites? Find the pair below that has the same relationship as the first pair.

CIRCUMNAVIGATE : SHIP ::
    a. postscript : letter
    b. antebellum : war
    c. orbit : satellite
    d. equivocate : speaker

ADVANCED WORD: CIRCUMSPECT

The word *circumspect* (sir-come-SPECT) contains the Latin stems *circum* (around) and *spect* (look). It means cautious, careful, on the lookout. *Circumspect* is an adjective, and so it can modify a noun or pronoun. You can have a circumspect spy, a circumspect answer, or a circumspect glance. In order to modify a pronoun, we would have to say something like, "She is circumspect." *Circumspect* is like a one-word poem (I call them *micropoems*) because it contains a little visual image of a careful person looking (*spect*) around (*circum*).

ADVANCED WORD: MALEVOLENCE

The noun *malevolence* is creepy. *Malevolence* means being mean, having bad (*mal*) will (*vol*) toward someone. *Malevolence* is the opposite of *benevolence*, which means kindness, and it can transform into the adjective *malevolent*. *Malevolence* was used by Shakespeare in his play *Macbeth* to describe "the malevolence of fortune." It was also used by Sir Walter Scott in *Ivanhoe* to describe

a "wrathful malevolence" and "any avaricious or malevolent noble."
(The word *avaricious* means greedy.) Charlotte Brontë referred to
"malevolent scorn" in her novel *Jane Eyre*. *Malevolence* also has
been used by Charles Dickens, by Joseph Conrad, and by William
Golding, who used the adverb form in *Lord of the Flies*: "He looked
malevolently at Jack." One of the best sentences comes from Harper
Lee, who wrote, in *To Kill a Mockingbird*, that "Inside the house
lived a malevolent phantom."

Which example of *malevolence* do you like the best?

WHO IS THAT WRITER?

Sir Walter Scott was born in Edinburgh, Scotland, on August
15, 1771. He was trained as a lawyer and became a legal official,
a profession that gave him time to write. Scott loved ballads and
legends. He wrote poetry in his early life, but in 1814 he began
writing novels and eventually wrote more than twenty. With the
profits from his novels, he built a great mansion in Abbotsford and
was named a baronet. Scott was the first great historical novelist,
and he influenced later writers such as James Fennimore Cooper,
Charles Dickens, and William Makepeace Thackeray. His 1819
classic *Ivanhoe* is one of the greatest tales about knights in all of
English literature. It is particularly notable for its descriptions of
how the Normans conquered Anglo Saxon England and for its
modern female characters. Together with the poet Robert Burns,
Scott helped to create Scottish literature.

CAESAR'S WORD SEARCH

In the puzzle, find the Latin-based English words.

```
T E M I B I C A M E R A L U Q B
S E R E N E E Q U I T A B L E E
O D I O U S T S E F I N A M M D
V X S U P E R F L U O U S T C N
L A N G U O R M A S O R C B U S
P D T T S I X E E R P C O I R A
O E C N A N E T N U O C U Q I R
S B A D E T A U N N A R E P U S
T R R C E O P R O D I G I O U S
E I D I U R L T I O R D A L A M
R E E F E T R O I R E T N A E T
I F D L B A E U Q S E T O R G U
O N U C I R C U M V E N T S Q P
R D C S U B T R A C T T X D U F
E L E E R D N E C S E D N O C X
D N U O F O R P B P R E D I C T
```

countenance	languor	preexist	deduce
profound	bicameral	superannuated	prelude
manifest	*sub rosa*	superfluous	subtract
prodigious	debrief	predict	serene
acute	grotesque	condescend	odious
circumvent	maladroit	posterior	equitable
anterior			

1. Which of these twenty-five words is most important?
2. Which of these words could apply to astronomy?
3. Which of these words are adjectives?
4. Which word has the most peaceful sound?
5. Can you use three of the words in one good sentence?

90

Caesar's Grammar · Parts of Speech

Identify the part of speech of each word.

1. Her idea was an **equitable** solution to the problem.

   _____

2. The tragedy was only a grim **prelude** to future disasters.

   _____

3. His **superfluous** explanation frustrated the weary soldiers.

   _____

4. Caesar easily **circumvented** the absurd prohibition.

   _____

5. The leader of the Gauls responded with **maladroit** tactics.

   _____

6. The **posterior** part of the wound was livid.

   _____

Caesar's MATHEMATICS

MMCDXXXIV maladroit barbarians retreated from the anterior area of the battle to the odious posterior section. There had been MMMDCC barbarians in the front lines when the battle began. How many maladroit barbarians remained on the front lines?

CAESAR'S SPANISH

A study of their stems shows that English and Spanish are related languages, using the same stems to make similar words.

stem	meaning	English / Spanish examples
circum	around	circumspect / circunspecto
mal	bad	malevolent / malévolo
post	after	posthumous / póstumo
equi	equal	equilateral / equilátero
ante	before	antecedent / antecedente

In these pairs of cognates, we continue to see the connection between English and Spanish vocabulary. In fact each of these words features two stems in a row, and in every case the Spanish word uses the same two Latin stems that the English word uses:

circum around, **spect** look
mal bad, **vol** will
post after, **hum** earth
equi equal, **lat** side
ante before, **cede** go

Even though English is at its foundation a Germanic language, English and Spanish are sibling languages in the way they both contain thousands of Latin-based words that use the same stems. Latin flooded into English with the 1066 invasion of England by the Normans, whose French descended from Latin.

PHARSALUS, AUGUST 9, 48 B.C.

Michael Clay Thompson

Not an equitable arrangement. Our 22,000 men,
standing in the grotesque Greek glare—long legions,
spears scraping the profound sky,
staring upslope at Pompey and his 45,000.
The ranks of the feeble Senate and People
of Rome, up there, waiting for us unabashed, a trap,
their anterior lines snap for battle, for the crash.
With clenched countenance Caesar said
that this was it. Victory or else. Else is bad.
Discipline is victory. Disarray is death.
Make them wish they'd circumvented this day.
Condescending Pompey's prodigious cavalry,
horses' manes in the Greek gusts, snorting
with acute fear and courage, eyes wide-dilated.
Pompey's legions wait, malevolent, serene.
Then we step forward, symphonic tramp
resounding, cramped formation, tramping higher
toward the odious moment. Closing. This is it.
Halfway, we pause. Not beginners, we.
Not maladroit rubes. We pause. Get a breath.
We're Caesar's legions. We've done this before.
The roar of Pompey's cavalry now manifest
on our right, thunder curving around from some
posterior spot in their position. It begins.

See map, page 29.

CAESAR'S PARAGRAPH

Let us write a **comparison** paragraph in which we compare Caesar to Pompey. The purpose of the paragraph is to show how Caesar and Pompey were different, so you will need to read about each of the two Romans and discover things that make them different. Perhaps one was rich and the other not. Perhaps they were trained in different ways. Perhaps one was more energetic or militarily brilliant. If you read thoughtfully, you will gradually find a small list of facts that show how Caesar and Pompey were different. Then write a short paragraph that blends our vocabulary into the sentences. The example of the comparison paragraph that appears in *Paragraph Town* is:

Queequack and Fishmeal are both ducks. They have strong beaks and love to paddle in the water with their webbed feet. That, however, is where their similarity ends, for Queequack is a Hooded Merganser with a great white crest on his head, while Mallard Fishmeal has a blue-green head and no crest at all. Furthermore, Queequack is a cosmopolitan duck, while Fishmeal has just arrived from the pond and has much to learn.

Your paragraph can be longer than this short example. Remember to use your vocabulary correctly, to avoid first person, to avoid contractions, and to use a serious, academic tone, not one that is chatty or cute.

JULIUS CAESAR, PART V

In 50 B.C. Caesar's five years in Gaul were finished. He had conquered Gaul, and with the symbiotic and equitable alliance of the Triumvirate over, Pompey and the condescending Roman Senate ordered Caesar to disband his legions and return to Rome. Caesar feared that Pompey viewed him as a dangerous rival, and indeed the unabashed Pompey accused him of treason.

In manifest defiance of the interdiction against maintaining his legions, the ambitious Caesar crossed the Rubicon River—then the northern border of Italy—with his Legion XIII, creating a prodigious civil war. Caesar is reported to have said, as he crossed the Rubicon, "The die is cast," a profound line from the Greek playwright Menander. Pompey and the Senate fled in disarray to Greece. Caesar had no fleet, so Pompey escaped. Caesar acutely took his legions to Spain and defeated Pompey's legions there. Caesar then assembled a fleet and pursued Pompey to Greece. On August 9 of 48 B.C., though outnumbered, Caesar defeated Pompey's legions at Pharsalus, with Pompey circumventing capture once more, this time fleeing to Egypt. Caesar took control of Rome.

Caesar became dictator of Rome, promoting himself to a second consulship. He chased Pompey to Egypt, but before he could capture Pompey, Pompey was grotesquely murdered, so Caesar remained in Egypt, choosing Cleopatra's side in an Egyptian civil war. Caesar could not marry Cleopatra because an odious Roman law permitted marriage only between Roman citizens.

From 48 to 45 B.C. Caesar pursued various military objectives, including the defeat of Cato, Pompey's senatorial ally, and the defeat of Pompey's sons in Spain. He also was elected as consul two more times.

PO

RUBICON

ARNO

CORSICA

TIBER

SARDINIA

SICILY

RIVERS OF ITALY

Review for Cumulative Quiz V

bi	two
sub	under
de	down
pre	before
super	over
un	not
inter	between
semi	half
dis	away
sym	together
circum	around
mal	bad
post	after
equi	equal
ante	before

bicameral	having two chambers
sub rosa	done in secret
debrief	to question someone
preexist	existing beforehand
superannuated	obsolete
countenance	facial expression
profound	deep
manifest	obvious
prodigious	huge
languor	weakness
unabashed	not embarrassed
interdict	a prohibition
semiannual	twice a year or half-yearly
disarray	disorganized or untidy
symbiotic	mutually beneficial
serene	calm
acute	sharp
grotesque	distorted
condescend	to patronize
odious	hateful
circumvent	get around
maladroit	clumsy, bungling
posterior	at the back, later
equitable	fair, impartial
anterior	near the front, earlier

THE GREEKS AND THE ROMANS

Thomas Milton Kemnitz

We speak of ancient Greece and Rome in one phrase, as though they are similar. The temptation to see them as one is compounded by the fact that they form the basis of a classical education, and it was their combined influence that shaped much of the thinking of the founders of the American Republic.

We should try to separate Greece and Rome because they made different lasting contributions to the English language, and they flourished at different times. The Greeks predated the Romans. Athens was an important city 650 years before Rome was founded. Athens reached its apex in power, influence, and culture while Rome was still a tiny town with mud streets, and Alexander the Great conquered most of the world worth taking when Rome was struggling to grow beyond its city walls.

The Romans admired Greek art, architecture, literature, and culture and copied much of what they saw from the antecedent civilization. Works considered to be the classics in Caesar's time had for the most part been written hundreds of years earlier by Greeks such as Homer, Plato, Aristotle, Sophocles, and Aesop.

At the left is the Acropolis with the Parthenon in Athens as seen serenely through Hadrian's Arch. Hadrian was one of the Roman emperors who was a benefactor to Greece.

Classic Words · Lesson VI

1. **exquisite**: beautifully made
2. **clamor**: outcry
3. **sublime**: lofty
4. **tremulous**: quivering
5. **allude**: indirectly refer to

EXQUISITE

The English adjective *exquisite* (and its adverb form *exquisitely*) comes to us from the Romans. In Latin *exquisitus* was a form of *exquirere*, to search out. When we say that something is exquisite, meaning that it is delicately beautiful or that it is exceptionally perfect, we are echoing the old Roman idea that an exquisite thing is something you do not see every day; it is something rare that you might search a long time to find. In literature we find *exquisite* modifying a surprising range of nouns: there are exquisite echoes, exquisite daughters, exquisite dishes, and exquisite manners. In James M. Barrie's novel *Peter Pan*, we read, "It was a girl called Tinker Bell exquisitely gowned in a skeleton leaf." In Joseph Conrad's *Lord Jim*, a butterfly spreads out dark bronze wings "with exquisite white veinings." In Stephen Crane's *The Red Badge of Courage*, the young soldier relaxes because "An exquisite drowsiness had spread through him." Most of the time, *exquisite* refers to things that are good, but sometimes it describes a bad thing that is extremely unusual, as when Jack London wrote in *The Call of the Wild* that "All the pain he had endured was as nothing compared with the exquisite agony of this." In Robert Louis Stevenson's *Dr. Jekyll and Mr. Hyde*, we read with a chill that "my blood was changed into something exquisitely thin and icy." What do you think Rachel Carson meant by her use of *exquisite* in *Silent Spring* when she wrote, "These include three of the thrushes whose songs are among the most exquisite of bird voices..."?

CLAMOR

The English noun *clamor* comes from the Latin *clamor* and the Latin verb *clamare*, to cry out. *Clamor* is sometimes spelled *clamour*. A clamor is no mild call; it is a loud outcry, a vociferous uproar, especially one that continues on vehemently. People *keep* clamoring. *Clamor* is a strong noun; it should not be wasted on any old holler. In English and American literature we find *clamor* used by William Golding, George Orwell, and Richard Wright. We find it used by modern writers such as Eudora Welty but also by Geoffrey Chaucer in 1385: "he maketh that the grete tour resoundeth of his youling and clamour." Notice the archaic (old) spellings of Chaucer's words. In *Macbeth* Shakespeare wrote that "the obscure bird clamoured the livelong night." The obscure bird, apparently, was an owl. In Walter Scott's 1820 novel *Ivanhoe*, we read about "the clamorous yells and barking of all the dogs in the hall." In *Tom Sawyer*, Mark Twain wrote about the "glad clamor of laughter." One of the most creative uses of *clamor* comes from *The Call of the Wild*, in which Jack London wrote that "He did not steal for joy of it because of the clamour of his stomach."

SUBLIME

If the English adjective *sublime* means noble or majestic (and it does), then why does it contain the Latin stem *sub* that means under? Well, in Rome, honored objects were placed up on or under (*sub*) the mantel (*limen*) where they could be seen, and so *sublime* means not down, but up, up under the mantel: up *sub* the *limen*. As many words do, *sublime* has a number of possible meanings, but they all connote a high, lofty state. *Sublime* may mean exalted, or inspiring, or grand. It may mean outstanding or supreme. Sometimes we use the word as a noun and refer to *the sublime*. Martin Luther King, Jr. wrote about "sublime courage." Mark Twain wrote about the "sublimity of his language," and Harriet Beecher Stowe wrote about "sublime heroism." In *Gulliver's Travels,* Jonathan Swift wrote of things that could be "comprehended only by a few persons of sublime genius." Stephen Crane described the courage of battle as a "temporary but sublime absence of selfishness." One of the most charming examples comes from Barrie's *Peter Pan*, where "now we are rewarded for our sublime faith in a mother's love."

TREMULOUS

Our English adjective *tremulous* is a direct descendant of the Latin *tremulus* and the verb *tremere*, to tremble. We call tremulous those who are trembling, who are shaking with tremors, or who are overly timid. Tremulous quivering, especially of the hand or voice, might be a result of fear, nervousness, or weakness, and it might have either a physical or psychological origin.

Tremulous has been a popular adjective among English and American writers for at least three centuries and has been used by Walter Scott, Nathaniel Hawthorne, Lewis Carroll, and Robert Louis Stevenson. Sometimes *tremulous* can describe the quivering of a musical note, as when Ralph Ellison wrote of "a tremulous, blue-toned chord." Sometimes *tremulous* describes the trembling of a voice, as when William Golding wrote that "Jack's voice went up, tremulous yet determined...." Lewis Carroll also used *tremulous* to describe the human voice in *Alice's Adventures in Wonderland*; Carroll wrote, "His voice has a timid and tremulous sound." Frances Hodgson Burnett used *tremulous* in her novel *The Secret Garden*, in which there were "two rabbits sitting up and sniffing with tremulous noses." In Barrie's *Peter Pan*, "John whispered tremulously." In Robert Louis Stevenson's *Kidnapped*, there was a "rather tremulous laughter." In *Leaves of Grass*, America's great poet Walt Whitman wrote that the "cattle stand and shake away flies with the tremulous shuddering of their hides."

What did Thackeray mean in *Vanity Fair* when he wrote, "he opened the letter rather tremulously"?

ALLUDE

To allude to something is to make an indirect reference to it, to hint. The English verb *allude* and its noun form *allusion* come to us from Latin, where we learn that the Latin verb *alludere* meant to play with. *Allude* is a word with spirit. Alluding to things, rather than directly stating them, gives us a playful option: we can call someone's attention to something without directly mentioning it. Alluding is a game of hints and guesses. In George Eliot's *Silas Marner* we read that "it was already four years since there had been any allusion to the subject between them." In Mary Shelley's novel *Frankenstein*, a character begs, "But until then, I conjure you, do not mention or allude to it." In his famous novel *A Passage to India*, E.M. Forster wrote, "They attacked one another with obscure allusions and had a silly quarrel." One of the very best sentences comes from Kenneth Grahame's children's classic *The*

Wind in the Willows, where we learn one of the most important differences between animals and people; Grahame wrote that "it is quite against animal etiquette to dwell on possible trouble ahead, or even to allude to it." All of the little animals, we infer, are optimists.

WHO IS THAT WRITER?

The author of *Alice in Wonderland*, known to us as Lewis Carroll, was really Charles Lutwidge Dodgson. Born in 1832 in Daresbury, Cheshire, England, Charles had seven sisters and three brothers. He was first educated at home, and at age seven he was already reading Bunyan's *The Pilgrim's Progress*, a very advanced book indeed. At twelve Dodgson went to private school in Richmond, and in 1845 he went to Rugby School, where his brilliance in mathematics was recognized. After college at Christ Church, Oxford, he accepted a position there as a lecturer in mathematics. In 1856 he published a poem, "Solitude," under the *nom de plume* (pen name) Lewis Carroll. He made friends with the new Oxford dean, Henry Liddell, who had a daughter named Alice. On a picnic Dodgson told Alice a story in which she was the main character, and she urged him to write it down. He did, offered it to MacMillan publishers under his pen name, and the rest is literary history. Dodgson taught at Christ Church until 1881, published papers in mathematics, and died of pneumonia in 1898.

sublime

WHAT IS THIS WRITER SAYING?

Discuss the meaning of the **bold** word in each of the following sentences:

From Bram Stoker's *Dracula*: "There was no place for words in his **sublime** misery."

From E.M. Forster's *A Passage to India*: "Aziz was **exquisitely** dressed, from tie-pin to spats."

From Richard Wright's *Native Son*: "His feelings **clamored** for an answer his mind could not give."

From James Joyce's *A Portrait of the Artist as a Young Man*: "A **tremulous** chill blew round his heart."

CAESAR'S MATHEMATICS

A sublime new aqueduct bringing water from the mountains to the city of Segovia in Roman Hispania requires MMCMLXXVIII clamoring Roman laborers for its construction. Only half of that number of workers can be found. How many workers are found?

CAESAR'S WORD SEARCH

In the puzzle, find the Latin-based English words.

```
T E X Q U I S I T E A V R B I D
T L R F O A L L U D E Q G S E G
Y E C N A N E T N U O C U H N O
R D E B R I E F X S B P S G F O
O S L F X V N B U Y E A R T T L
I T I S G T R O R R B O R N S M
R S Y Y S Y I O A A T E E B B A
E I A H P D M N N E M V S B X L
T X M T O A N U S U M U P D S A
S E M O L U B Q L U B R R I E D
O E O C A Q U O C L L B O S R R
P R Q T Q E U R I M Q R F A E O
E P E S S S I M B Q A L O R N I
X D O D U C E R P T F A U R E T
C I N T E R D I C T P E N A D F
R O U G N A L E H A I E D Y A Y
```

preexist	debrief	superannuated	languor
countenance	profound	unabashed	interdict
disarray	serene	grotesque	odious
circumvent	posterior	maladroit	exquisite
clamor	sublime	tremulous	allude

1. Which of these words has the harshest sound?
2. Which of these words has the most syllables?
3. Which of these words are adjectives?
4. Which word would be good to use in a joke?
5. Which word is the hardest to learn?

Caesar's Synonyms

Here are words that are similar to the words in our list, but are they exactly the same in meaning? Or are they slightly different? For each word on our list, look up any synonym that you do not know, then pick one, and carefully explain the difference between it and our word.

exquisite: dainty, elaborate, graceful, fine, delicate, refined, glamorous, beautiful, intricate

clamor: babel, hubbub, din, uproar, bellow, clatter, blare, pandemonium, yell, racket, bawl, caterwaul, cacophony

sublime: ideal, heavenly, utopian, perfect, idyllic, Arcadian, empyrean, paradisiac, Elysian, Edenic, lofty

tremulous: quivery, trembling, shivering, aquiver, shaky, wobbly, anxious, edgy, frightened, timid, nervous, fearful

allude: mention, comment, touch on, refer to, point out, note, bring up, observe, animadvert, advert, remark

Caesar's Spanish

Everywhere we turn, language reveals to us that modern English and modern Spanish are both descendants of ancient Latin:

Latin	Spanish	English
exquisitus	exquisito	exquisite
clamor	clamor	clamor
sublimis	sublime	sublime
tremulus	trémulo	tremulous
alludere	aludir	allude

110

CAESAR'S REWRITES

Here are some sentences from famous books. In each case, rewrite the sentence into more ordinary words. Example from Marjorie Rawlings's *The Yearling*: "A languor crept over him." The rewrite: Little by little, he began to feel lazy.

From Herman Melville's *Moby Dick*: "For the most part, in this tropic whaling life, a **sublime** uneventfulness invests you; you hear no news; read no gazettes."

From Jack London's *The Call of the Wild*: "Every part, brain and body, nerve tissue and fibre, was keyed to the most **exquisite** pitch."

From Kenneth Grahame's *The Wind in the Willows*: "It is quite against animal etiquette to dwell on possible trouble ahead, or even to **allude** to it."

From Richard Wright's *Native Son*: "His feelings **clamored** for an answer his mind could not give."

allude

CAESAR'S GRAMMAR · PARTS OF SENTENCE

In the first five lessons, we studied the eight parts of speech in order to understand vocabulary usage. We now can extend these ideas by studying the second level of grammar, the parts of sentence. In this second level, we learn what the different kinds of words do in sentences—how words make ideas. There are only five parts of sentence.

1. **SUBJECT** (subj.) The subject of the sentence is the noun or pronoun that the sentence is about: **Caesar** attacked at dawn.

2. **PREDICATE** (AVP or LVP) The *simple* predicate is the verb. The *complete* predicate is the verb and all of the words that belong to it. We will focus on the simple predicate: Caesar **attacked** at dawn. The verb can be an *action* verb, Caesar **attacked**, or it can be a *linking* verb: Caesar **was** the consul.

We will use AVP to stand for action verb predicate, and LVP to stand for linking verb predicate.

3. **DIRECT OBJECT** (D.O.) If the verb is action, then the action might be done on a direct object—a noun or pronoun that receives the action: Caesar attacked the barbarian **army**.

4. **INDIRECT OBJECT** (I.O.) If there is a direct object, then there might be an indirect object between the action verb and the direct object. Caesar gave the **Gauls** a warning.

5. **SUBJECT COMPLEMENT** (S.C.) If there is a linking verb, then there might be a subject complement that is linked in an equation with the subject: Caesar was the **consul**.

Study the first five examples on the following page, and see if you can complete the final three. Notice that the object of a preposition cannot also be a D.O. or an I.O. For much more about the parts of sentence, see the presentation in *Grammar Town*.

1. The **exquisite** building impressed the Germans.
   adj.   adj.   n.   v.   adj.   n.
         subj.   AVP   D.O.

2. The senate **clamored** for a new treaty.
   adj.   n.   v.   prep.   adj.   adj.   n.
     subj.   AVP

3. A **tremulous** breeze gave the legion relief.
   adj.   adj.   n.   v.   adj.   n.   n.
       subj.   AVP   I.O.   D.O.

4. The speech was a **sublime** moment in Caesar's career.
   adj.   n.   v.   adj.   adj.   n.   prep.   n.   n.
     subj.   LVP   S.C.

5. Caesar indirectly **alluded** to the former Triumvirate.
   n.   adv.   v.   prep.   adj.   adj.   n.
   subj.   AVP

6. The **maladroit** governor was an old friend of Caesar.

7. Caesar easily **circumvented** the **superannuated** law.

8. The **grotesque** situation gave Caesar a headache.

Notice that our ideas tend to express actions or equations, and that there are standard patterns: subj.-AVP-D.O., subj.-AVP-I.O.-D.O., and subj.-LVP-S.C. Notice how important nouns are.

CAESAR'S ANTONYMS

For each of the words in this lesson, think of a word that means the opposite, known as an *antonym*.

1. **exquisite**
2. **clamor**
3. **sublime**
4. **tremulous**
5. **allude**

Are there any words in this list that have no antonyms? Are there any for which it is difficult to think of an antonym? Why?

CAESAR'S ANALOGIES

Analogies are about relationships. Find a second pair of words that have the same relationship to each other as the first pair has. Remember that it sometimes helps to put the two words into a sentence that makes the relationship clear.

SUBLIME : PEDESTRIAN ::
  a. amiable : peevish
  b. clamor : hubbub
  c. perplex : mystery
  d. clamor : riot

TREMULOUS : FEAR ::
  a. clamorous : anger
  b. incredulous : gullible
  c. sublime : noble
  d. amiable : person

DUM SPIRO SPERO.

While I breathe,
I hope.

- Cicero

SOUTH TO CARTHAGE

Michael Clay Thompson

Acute clamor in the streets—babble—
he knew it was trouble. Then the rabble,
grotesque barbarians massing on the hill,
a thousand yards past the walls, after loot,
malevolent, painted countenances, garrulous,
more, more, more, until they darkened
the hill like an odious disarray of vermin.
Voices in the Forum tremulous or mute,
distorted, fear manifest in accusations, hate,
the profound delusion of circumventing fate.
Not equitable, he gathered wife and son,
with *sub rosa* interdictions against talk. Run.
Come now, say nothing. Don't walk,
run. Too late to debrief. Don't wait.
Through the streets, to the docks
and into the boat, langorously rocking.
Cast off, the aft sun a sublime red glow
lowering over the glimmery city, they sailed
south into the prodigious Tyrrhenian night,
fast, Rome posterior, ropes creaking tight
and the maladroit flap of the sail, night veil,
the exquisite splash of water washing the bow,
moonless black wrap of serene stars, dashing
straight for Carthage, the antecedent enemy.
Unabashed he would beg Carthagenian mercy,
abject, kicked, like a convict.

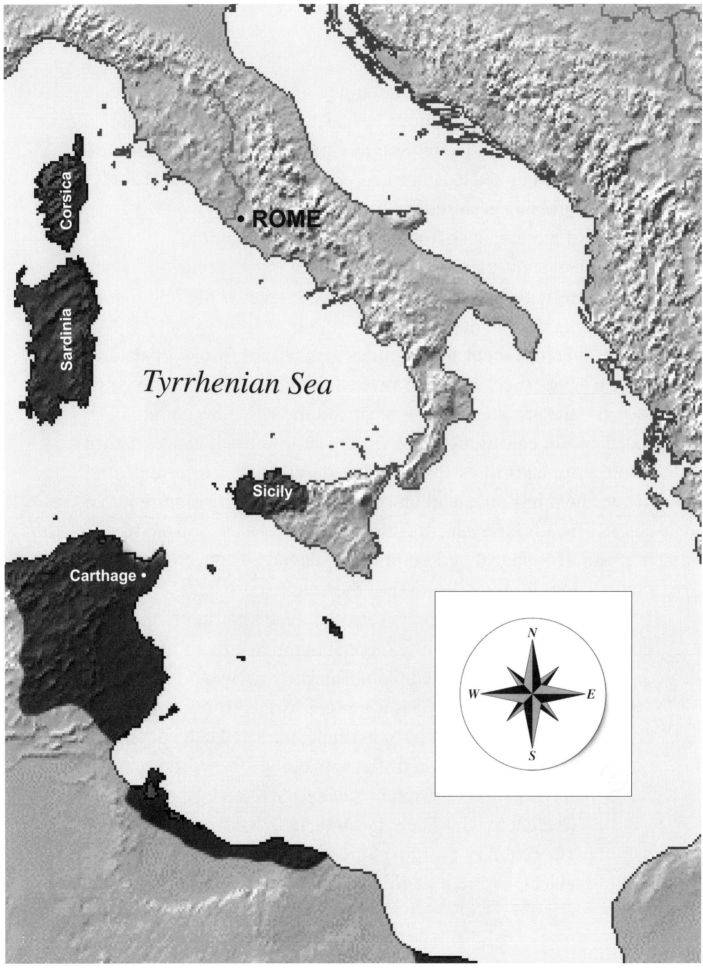

Corsica

Sardinia

• ROME

Tyrrhenian Sea

Sicily

Carthage •

N
W   E
S

JULIUS CAESAR, PART VI

After Caesar vanquished Pompey's sons in Spain, the Senate piled honors upon him. Though he had profound enemies in Rome, he pardoned them, and clamorous celebrations honored his victories.

Caesar returned to Rome in 45 B.C., and the city held tributes to him, including grotesque wild beast hunts involving 400 lions. Armies of war prisoners fought in the Circus Maximus.

Caesar soon drew up a will, naming his grandnephew Octavian as his heir, with Marcus Junius Brutus to receive the inheritance if Octavian were to die first.

Concerned about the tremulous weakness of Rome's maladroit central government and the way Romans manifestly circumvented the law, Caesar created a new constitution for the empire. The focus of the constitution was on crushing the odious resistance in the provinces to establish order, on creating a strong central government in Rome, and on connecting the entire empire into a single, efficient governmental structure. Caesar accomplished much of this first by defeating Pompey and second by concentrating his power and reforming the laws of the empire.

His sublime legislative reforms included putting term limits on the governors of provinces, conducting a census to make the distribution of grain more equitable, and providing land for 15,000 veterans of his legions. Caesar's most exquisite reform was to create a new calendar. Rome had a superannuated calendar based on the phases of the moon, and after consulting with the astronomer Sosigenes of Alexandria, Caesar replaced it with an Egyptian-style, sun-based calendar. This made a year of 365.25 days, with an extra leap day on February every four years. Caesar's Julian calendar would serve the Western world for more than five centuries.

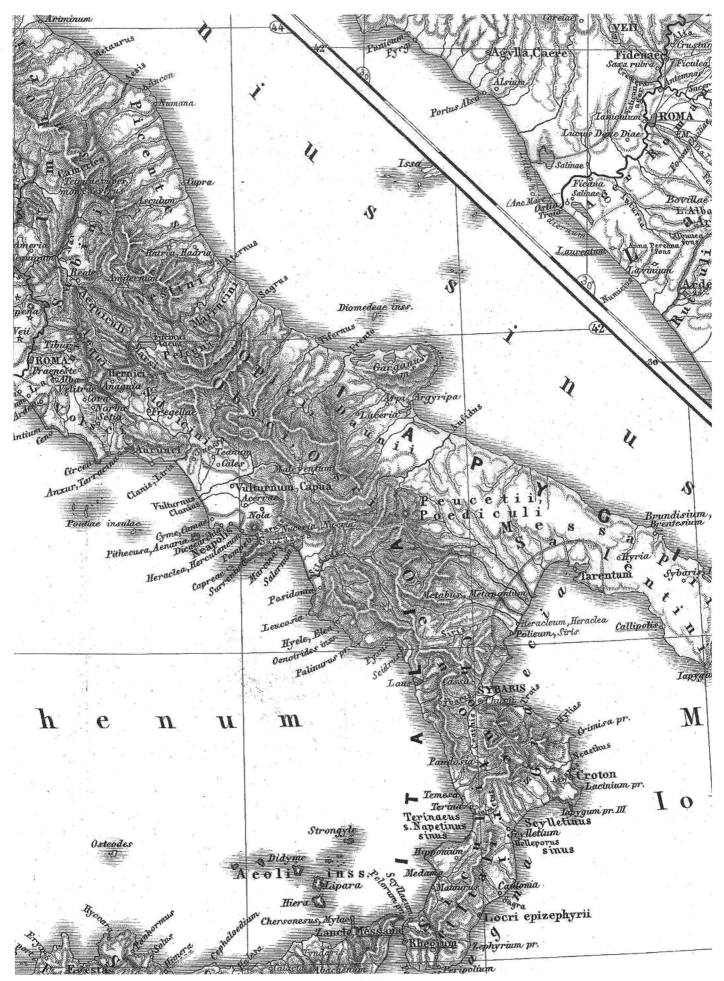

Ariminum
Metaurus
Ancon
Numana

Picentes
Camertes
Tetricae mons, mont Severus
Asculum
Cupra

Truentum
Hatria, Hadria
Interamnia
Aternus
Sagrus

Reate
Ameria
Teguzgam
Vestini
Marrucini

Diomedeae inss.

Tibur
ROMA
Praeneste
Alba
Velitrae Anagnia
Cora
Norba Setia
Fregellae
Aurunci
Suessa Teanum Cales

Garganus m.

Arpi Argyripa
Luceria
Aufidus
A P Y

Peucetii,
Poediculi

Circeii
Anxur, Tarracina
Clanis, Liris
Vulturnus
Clanius

Vulturnum, Capua
Acerrae
Nola
Nuceria, Nucaria

Messa
Brundisium,
Brentesium

Hyria

Tarentum
Sybaris

Pontiae insulae
Cyme, Cumae
Pithecusa, Aenaria
Dicaearchia
Neapolis

Heraclea, Herculaneum
Capreae
Surrentum
Pompeji
Salernum

Posidonia
Metabus, Metapontium

Calipolis

Heracleum, Heraclea
Polieum, Siris
Siris

Leucosia
Hyele, Elea
Oenotrides inss.
Palinurus pr.

Laus

Cassa

SYBARIS
Thurii Copia

Iapygia

M

h e n u m

Hylias
Grimisa pr.
Neaethus

Pandosia
Croton
Lacinium pr.

Temesa
Terina
Terinaeus
s. Napetinus
sinus

Iapygium pr. III
Scylletinus
Scylletium
Melaporus sinus

Strongyle

Osteodes

Hipponium
Medama

Didyme
Aeoli inss.
Lipara
Hiera

Terina

Metaurus
Caulonia
Locri epizephyrii

Hyccara
Panhormus
Solus

Chersonesus, Mylae
Lanche Messana
Rhegium
Zephyrium pr.

Egesta
Himera
Cephaloedium
Tyndaris
Alaesa Abacaenum
Peripolium

VEII
Cremera
Crustu
Ficulea
Agylla, Caere
Fidenae
Saxa rubra

Issa
Alsium
Portus Alsi

Ianiculum
ROMA

Lucus Deae Diae

Ficana
Salinae
Salinae

Laurentum

Lavinium
Ardea

Io

M

119

Review for Cumulative Quiz VI

bi	two	**dis**	away	
sub	under	**sym**	together	
de	down	**circum**	around	
pre	before	**mal**	bad	
super	over	**post**	after	
un	not	**equi**	equal	
inter	between	**ante**	before	
semi	half			

bicameral	having two chambers
sub rosa	done in secret
debrief	to question someone
preexist	existing beforehand
superannuated	obsolete
countenance	facial expression
profound	deep
manifest	obvious
prodigious	huge
languor	weakness
unabashed	not embarrassed
interdict	a prohibition
semiannual	twice a year or half-yearly
disarray	disorganized or untidy
symbiotic	mutually beneficial
serene	calm
acute	sharp
grotesque	distorted
condescend	to patronize
odious	hateful
circumvent	get around
maladroit	clumsy, bungling
posterior	at the back, later
equitable	fair, impartial
anterior	near the front, earlier
exquisite	beautifully made
clamor	outcry
sublime	lofty
tremulous	quivering
allude	indirectly refer to

CONCRETE

Thomas Milton Kemnitz

The Romans were far superior to the Greeks in organization, engineering, and construction, and they erected far larger buildings than any the Greeks could envision. Two Roman innovations in combination enabled prodigious construction projects. One was the development of concrete, and the other was its use in arches. Small arches had been used by various cultures for millennia; the Roman innovation was to hold together huge arches with concrete. Because arches bear weight well, the Romans could build on a massive scale. Everywhere there is a Roman ruin, there are evidences of the arch and/or concrete.

In the Pantheon in Rome, the most complete existing building from the Roman Empire, we see the use of concrete in the extraordinary dome. The dome rose to a central opening—called an *oculus* by the Romans—which let in light. The dome was made entirely of concrete, and it was the largest dome anyone in the world was able to make for the next 1,300 years. It still stands today, 1,900 years after it was first constructed; at 142 feet across and 142 feet high, it is the largest unreinforced concrete dome anyone has ever constructed.

Note how each part of the roof is inset to form an interesting design that uses less concrete; the lower weight reduces the load on the building. This is called a coffered ceiling.

ALEA IACTA EST.
The die is cast.
- Julius Caesar

LATIN STEMS · LESSON VII

stem	meaning	modern examples
aqua	water	aquatic, aqueduct, aquarium
audi	hear	auditory, audience, audiophile
scrib	write	scribe, inscribe, describe
cede	go	recede, precede, secede
cise	cut	excise, incisive, incisors

AQUA means water. An *aquarium* is a tank of water with fish in it. *Aquatic* means of the water, and an *aqueduct* was built by the Romans to bring water to the city.

AUDI means hear. Your *auditory* nerves help you hear. An *audience* will hear you, and an *audiophile* is a lover of stereo equipment.

SCRIB means write. A *scribe* is one who writes things down. To *inscribe* is to write something inside a book, and to *describe* is to write down a description.

CEDE means go. A flood goes back when it *recedes*. Someone *precedes* you when he or she goes first, and the South tried to *secede* from the Union in the Civil War by going apart.

CISE means cut. To *excise* is to cut out. To say something *incisive* is to say something that cuts into the issue, and *incisors* are teeth that cut.

dio tape audi ologist

ac cede aqua marine

ante cede nt con cise

ecede audit aqua tic

gy ex cise aqua relle

le re cede aqua cade

scribe aqua phobia

pre cede audi ometer

e aqua batics scribe

ole inter cede in cise

in scribe aqua lung

cede nts audio book

on criti cise aqua tint

con cede sub aqua tic

dio metric describe

NONFICTION WORDS

Here are five advanced nonfiction words. You will not hear them in daily conversation, but you will encounter them in your future academic life. Each word is based on one of the stems in this lesson.

stem	word	definition
aqua	**aquamarine**	light bluish-green
audi	**audible**	able to be heard
scrib	**proscribed**	forbidden
cede	**concede**	to surrender, admit defeat
cise	**incised**	cut into

AQUAMARINE is an adjective or a noun that refers to a light bluish-green color, such as we might see in the Mediterranean Sea.

AUDIBLE is an adjective that refers to sounds, such as voices, that can be heard. A noise you cannot hear is inaudible.

PROSCRIBED is an adjective that means forbidden or banished. We also see the word as a verb, as when an emperor proscribes certain acts, often defining them as criminal. As a young man, Caesar was proscribed and condemned.

CONCEDE is a verb that means to surrender, to admit defeat, or even to admit that you are wrong. The losing candidate in an election calls the winning candidate to concede.

INCISED is an adjective that refers to marks, designs, or words that are cut into something, such as wood or stone. The ancient Romans incised designs into metal and stone.

CAESAR'S ANALOGY

The first two words are related to each other in a special way. Is one before the other? Is one inside the other? Are they opposites? Find the pair below that has the same relationship as the first pair.

SCRIBE : WRITES ::
a. audience : hears
b. audiophile : stereo
c. incisive : speech
d. aquarium : fish

ADVANCED WORD: AQUEDUCT

The noun *aqueduct* (awk-wa-dukt) contains the stems *aqua* (water) and *duct* (lead). The Romans built aqueducts, which were long channels that carried water from the mountain streams all the way down to Rome in the valley below. Some of the aqueducts were huge and made of rows of arches on top of other rows of arches. At the very top of the aqueduct, above all of the arches, was the channel where the water flowed. Some of the Roman aqueducts are still standing today, 2,000 years after they were built. One reason they were so strong is that the Romans invented concrete, which helped the rocks hold together over long periods of time.

ADVANCED WORD: INCISIVE

One word that you are likely to read or hear is the adjective *incisive*. From the Latin *incisivus*, *incisive* usually refers to something that someone says, and it means just what its stems suggest: cutting in. A comment or response that really cuts directly into the heart of the matter is incisive. One writer who loved this adjective was the great American novelist Henry James. In his novel *The American*, James wrote, "It was in this incisive strain that Mrs. Tristram moralised over Newman's so-called neglect." We also read, "You know how terribly incisive she is sometimes," and James described how a character, "dropped a series of softly-incisive comments upon her fellow-guests." One writer for younger readers who used the word *incisive* was James M. Barrie, the author of *Peter Pan*; Barrie wrote that "The order came sharp and incisive." Joseph Conrad used *incisive* several times in *Lord Jim*, and James Watson, a famous scientist who helped discover DNA, the chemical basis of life, wrote that "the chemists never provided anything incisive about the nucleic acids." Nucleic acids are important chemicals that are in the center, called the nucleus, of each cell in our bodies.

Which of these examples of *incisive* do you like the best?

How many different meanings of *incisive* do you see?

WHO IS THAT WRITER?

James D. Watson, whose middle name was Dewey, was born in 1928 in Chicago. He received a Ph.D. degree from Indiana University in 1950. In 1955 he began teaching at Harvard. In 1962 he and Francis Crick, a British scientist, received the Nobel Prize for discovering the molecular structure of the DNA molecule, a structure of atoms that is the basis of life on earth. In 1968 Watson wrote *The Double Helix*, telling the story of his work with Crick and how they made their great discovery.

CAESAR'S WORD SEARCH

In the puzzle, find the Latin-based English words.

```
L C E R Q P R O F O U N D G A E
T I O R D A L A M A N I F E S T
L A N G U O R E M X P T F C B D
O D I O U S M C S U O N T T N T
T D D E T A U N N A R E P U S P
P E E X S E P A P A L V E S Q R
R S N R E E R N R F E M A U D P
O I I O D N E E E D U U O N O
D C R I U E D T E I E C D U E S
I N A R L R I N X R C R I L C T
G I M E E E C U I B N I B F S E
I F A T R S T O S E O C L R E R
O X U N P N P C T D C S E E D I
U I Q A D E B I R C S O R P N O
S U A E E L B A T I U Q E U O R
O G R O T E S Q U E L N A S C M
```

countenance	languor	preexist	audible
profound	aquamarine	superannuated	prelude
manifest	concede	superfluous	proscribed
prodigious	debrief	predict	serene
incised	grotesque	condescend	odious
circumvent	maladroit	posterior	equitable
anterior			

1. Which of these words has the softest sound?
2. Which of these words might you hear in an art class?
3. Which of these words can be verbs?
4. Which word has the scratchiest sound?
5. Can you use three of the words in one good sentence?

CAESAR'S GRAMMAR · PARTS OF SENTENCE

Study the first four examples; then see if you can do the second four the same way.

1. Yes, the enemies of Caesar finally **conceded** defeat.
   interj. adj. n. prep. n. adv. v. n.
   subj. AVP D.O.

   Note: The direct object will always be a noun or pronoun.

---

2. His words were clearly **audible** throughout the Forum.
   adj. n. v. adv. adj. prep. adj. n.
   subj. LVP S.C.

   Note: The subject complement can be a noun, pronoun, or adjective.

---

3. The new constitution **proscribed** the superannuated practice.
   adj. adj. n. v. adj. adj. n.
   subj. AVP D.O.

---

4. Caesar gave Pompey the exquisite **aquamarine** ring.
   n. v. n. adj. adj. adj. n.
   subj. AVP I.O. D.O.

   Note: The indirect object will always be between the action verb and the direct object.

---

5. The mason **incised** the name of the legion into the column.

---

6. A **tremulous** movement in the trees warned Caesar.

---

7. Caesar easily **circumvented** the blockade of the Gauls.

---

8. The first sign of dissatisfaction was the loud **clamor**.

A ROMAN FACT

The Emperor Octavian, called Augustus, was among the greatest of the Roman emperors. When he died, the Roman Empire covered 3,340 square miles, an area larger than the continental United States. This territory was more than a hundred times larger than the Roman Empire before the Punic Wars with Carthage. Augustus was described as having the most serene countenance anyone had ever seen.

CAESAR'S SPANISH

English and Spanish share many stems from ancient Latin. Look at the pairs of stems in these words:

stem	*meaning*	*English / Spanish examples*
aqua	water	aqueduct / acueducto
audi	hear	auditory / auditorio
scrib	write	inscribe / inscribir
cede	go	intercede / interceder
cise	cut	incisive / incisivo

CAESAR'S MATHEMATICS

In the clamorous debate, XXXIV ideas were not conceded, CXIII were proscribed, and LVI were too inaudible to be considered. The rest of the DXXIII ideas were approved. How many were approved?

OCTAVIAN

Michael Clay Thompson

This is the prodigious empire Octavian built.

These are the exquisite roads sublime
that link the prodigious empire Octavian built.

These are legions, so serene,
that tramp the exquisite roads routine,
that link the prodigious empire Octavian built.

These are the tremulous Gauls in the hills
that watch the legions, all serene,
that march the exquisite roads routine,
that link the prodigious empire Octavian built.

This is the langourous traitor, debriefed
on the clamorous Gauls and their manifest griefs,
that watch the legions so serene,
that march the exquisite roads routine,
that link the prodigious empire Octavian built.

This is the equitable law of the land
that protects the odious man, debriefed,
that laughs at the tremulous Gauls in the leaves,
that watch the legions, serene in peace,
that tramp the exquisite roads at ease
that link the prodigious empire Octavian built.

These are condescending scribes
who copy the law profound, revised,
that protects the traitor, now despised,
that betrays the Gauls in leaves unseen,
that watch the legions all serene,
that slog the Roman roads between
the cities of the prodigious empire Octavian built.

These are the words in stone incised
the words of the law profound, revised—
scrawled by condescending scribes—
that protect the unabashed snitch, who tries
to betray the Gauls and all their griefs
who watch the legions all serene,
that trudge the exquisite roads policing
the prodigious empire Octavian built.

This is the hawk above the wind
that wings the empire, end to end,
with vision acute, perception wise,
high above the words incised,
above the condescending scribes
and the maladroit traitor and his lies
who betrays the oppressed Gauls proscribed,
who watch the legions march serene
down the Roman roads between
the cities that express the dream
of the prodigious empire Octavian built.

JULIUS CAESAR, PART VII

After he reformed the superannuated Roman calendar, Caesar turned his attention to sublime matters that clamored for resolution. Caesar ordered Corinth and Carthage, which had been destroyed in 146 B.C. after the Third Punic War, to be rebuilt and established as Roman colonies. He created a police force that distributed land to the veterans of his legions. To increase the unity and diminish the disarray of the Roman provinces, Caesar increased the equitable citizenship rights of people throughout the Roman world, allowing them to be considered Romans rather than as maladroit, tremulous subjects.

Never languorous, Caesar had plans to construct a huge temple to Mars and to build a prodigious Roman library that would equal the exquisite library in Alexandria, founded by Alexander the Great near the Nile delta. Caesar wanted to develop Ostia, on the coast of the Tyrrhenian Sea sixteen miles downstream the Tiber from Rome, into a great port for Mediterranean commerce, and he wanted his engineers to cut a canal through the Isthmus of Corinth, connecting the aquamarine waters of the Ionian and Aegean seas and circumventing the need to sail completely around Greece in the high seas of the Mediterranean.

Caesar also planned military invasions of Dacia and the Persian empire of Parthia. He particularly wanted to defeat the odious Parthians because in 53 B.C. they had defeated Crassus's legions at the battle of Carrhae in Mesopotamia.

History must concede that these plans, however, were never finished because in 44 B.C., on the Ides of March (March 15), Caesar was grotesquely assassinated as he entered the Senate.

DACIA

BLACK

• Ostia

ADRIATIC

TYRRHENIAN

AEGEAN

Carrhae •

IONIAN

PARTHIA

Corinth •

• Carthage

• Alexandria

REVIEW FOR CUMULATIVE QUIZ VII

bi	two	**dis**	away
sub	under	**sym**	together
de	down	**circum**	around
pre	before	**mal**	bad
super	over	**post**	after
un	not	**equi**	equal
inter	between	**ante**	before
semi	half		

bicameral	having two chambers	*sub rosa*	done in secret
debrief	to question someone	**preexist**	existing beforehand
superannuated	obsolete	**countenance**	facial expression
profound	deep	**manifest**	obvious
prodigious	huge	**languor**	weakness
unabashed	not embarrassed	**interdict**	a prohibition
semiannual	twice a year or half-yearly	**disarray**	disorganization or disorder
symbiotic	mutually beneficial	**serene**	calm
acute	sharp	**grotesque**	distorted
condescend	to patronize	**odious**	hateful
circumvent	get around	**maladroit**	clumsy, bungling
posterior	at the back, later	**equitable**	fair, impartial
anterior	near the front, earlier	**exquisite**	beautifully made
clamor	outcry	**sublime**	lofty
tremulous	quivering	**allude**	indirectly refer to
aquamarine	light bluish-green	**audible**	able to be heard
proscribed	forbidden	**concede**	surrender, admit defeat
incised	cut in		

THE DORIC COLUMN

Thomas Milton Kemnitz

The Greeks used columns to hold up the roofs of buildings. A Roman engineer and builder named Vitruvius wrote a treatise on architecture, *De Architectura*, which is the only ancient writing on architecture that has come down to us. He described three distinct Greek styles of buildings and laid out the rules for those styles: Doric, Ionian, and Corinthian. The Romans deliberately followed the preexisting Greek styles of columns.

The Doric is the oldest of the three Greek orders. It was developed in the seventh century B.C., a little after the time Rome was founded. It is the simplest and sturdiest of the Greek orders. The exquisite Parthenon was built in the Doric style. The Doric column sits directly on the platform or floor of the building rather than on a base. The column itself has twenty parallel flutes cut into it, and it is topped by a smooth capital that flares from the column to meet a square abacus at the intersection with the horizontal beam that the column carries. Vitruvius provided a measurement of columns in terms of their height as a ratio of their base; at a height of six or seven times the diameter of its base, the

Doric column was the stoutest of the columns. The columns pictured on the left are in Pompeii and were built in the Doric style. Many Roman-built columns still standing are now bare of their fluting.

PATRIA EST COMMUNIS OMNIUM PARENS.

The fatherland is the common parent of us all.

-Cicero

CLASSIC WORDS · LESSON VIII

1. **placid**: calm
2. **singular**: unique
3. **amiable**: friendly
4. **incredulous**: skeptical
5. **perplex**: confuse

PLACID

The peaceful English adjective *placid* means tranquil, calm, untroubled. We are pleased by the quiet and undisturbed feeling of a placid environment or a placid mind, and this is to be expected because *placid* comes to us from the Romans' word *placidus*, a relative of *placere*, to please. *Placid* has variations, such as the adverb *placidly* and the noun *placidity*, but it also has subtle word connections that may go unnoticed; when we *placate* someone, we make him placid, unless he is *implacable*.

Placid has been used by modern writers such as Sylvia Plath and Pearl Buck, by nineteenth century writers such as George Eliot, Harriet Beecher Stowe, and Charlotte Brontë, and by eighteenth century writers such as Mary Wollstonecraft.

Harper Lee wrote about a "placid week." Martin Luther King, Jr., wrote about a "placid spring," and Marjorie Kinnan Rawlings wrote about a "deep and placid river." In Grahame's *The Wind in the Willows,* there are "lakes so blue and placid" and a face that "wore a placid, satisfied expression." What do you think this means, when we describe a face as placid? In James M. Barrie's *Peter Pan,* we read that "Even then Mrs. Darling was placid." In *Dracula* Bram

Stoker wrote, "I found Renfield sitting placidly in his room with his hands folded, smiling benignly." Long John Silver, in Robert Louis Stevenson's *Treasure Island*, is seen "standing placidly by." And in Sir Walter Scott's *Ivanhoe* we learn that Cedric "was in no very placid state of mind." In Mary Shelley's novel *Frankenstein*, there is a sentence that contains our words *exquisite* and *placid* and also the great word *verdure*, which means greenery. Shelley wrote that a river, "the lovely Isis, which flows beside it through meadows of exquisite verdure, is spread forth into a placid expanse of waters."

SINGULAR

The origin of the English adjective *singular*, though not simple, is *simple*. That is, the dictionary traces *singular* back to the Latin *singularis* and tells us to look up *single*, which is traced back to the Latin *singulus*, at which point the dictionary tells us to look up *simple*, which traces back to the Latin *simplus/simplex*, at which point the dictionary tells us to look up *simplex*, which turns out to be Latin for one-fold, with *sim* meaning one and *plex* meaning fold. The meaning of *singular* is what you would expect: single in nature. Something that is singular can be unique, extraordinary, strange, or exceptional.

In Frances Hodgson Burnett's novel *The Secret Garden*, "Colin had read about a great many singular things and was somehow a very convincing sort of boy." Burnett also wrote that "A wind was rising and making a singular, wild, low, rushing sound." In *The Wind in the Willows*, we read that "Toad is busily arraying himself in those singularly hideous habiliments so dear to him." In Kingston's translation of Wyss's *The Swiss Family Robinson*, there is "the most singular-looking creature I ever beheld." Robert Louis Stevenson, in *Kidnapped*, wrote that "both Mr. Riach and the captain were singularly patient." In *Gulliver's Travels*, Jonathan Swift wrote that Gulliver had "never till then seen a race of mortals so singular in their shapes, habits, and countenances."

AMIABLE

The adjective *amiable* comes from the Latin *amicabilis*, friendly, which came from the Latin *amicus*, friend, which was related to the Latin *amare*, to love. *Amiable* means friendly, good-natured, or agreeable. The word is one of the greatest English classic words; it has been in constant literary use since the 1300s, when Chaucer used it in *The Canterbury Tales*. It also was used by some of the other great early writers in English literature, such as William Shakespeare, Christopher Marlowe, and John Milton, who wrote the great epic poem *Paradise Lost*. In modern times it has been used by Toni Morrison, who won the Nobel prize for literature. Kenneth Grahame used it to describe "your amiable friend Mole," and Marjorie Kinnan Rawlings used it in *The Yearling* to describe Jody's mother: "Jody had never seen her so amiable." Rawlings also described bear cubs: "The cubs made now and then an amiable talking." In *Peter Pan,* Peter calls Tink's name amiably. In Harper Lee's novel *To Kill a Mockingbird*, we read that "He waited in amiable silence," and Jonathan Swift used *amiable* in his famous *Gulliver's Travels*, a great book for children that can be reread all of one's life; Swift wrote that "truth appeared so amiable to me that I determined upon sacrificing everything to it."

An interesting sentence comes from novelist Henry James, who used *amiable* in his 1876 novel *The American*. James also used our word *countenance* and the interesting word *saturnine*, which means distant and remote, like the planet Saturn. James wrote that "His countenance, by daylight, had a sort of amiably saturnine cast." Does it seem strange to you that someone could be saturnine and amiable at the same time?

INCREDULOUS

The dubious adjective *incredulous*, meaning full of disbelief, reached the English language from the shores of Italy. In other words, like the other words we have studied, *incredulous* comes from ancient Latin, where it was the Roman word *incredulus*. In 2,000 years, we have added one *o* to the word.

Incredulous is part of a great family of words in English, including *credulous*, *credulity*, *incredulity*, *credible*, *incredible*, *credit*, *creditable*, *credo*, *discredit*, *creed*, and even *miscreant*. The key to all of these words is that the stem *cred* means belief.

It is interesting that *incredulous* comes to English later than most words we have studied. Even the *Oxford English Dictionary*, which often traces words from the thirteenth century, gives no examples of usage before the late 1500s. The first use of *incredulous* in the books we have mentioned is in Jane Austen's *Pride and Prejudice*, which was not published until 1813. In that book there is an "audience not merely wondering but incredulous," a "smile of affected incredulity," and a moment when Elizabeth looks "at her sister with incredulous solicitude." *Solicitude* is concern.

In Grahame's *The Wind in the Willows*, something happens "full in view of the astonished and hitherto incredulous Mole." In the great American philosophical essay, *Walden*, Henry David Thoreau wrote that "my friends used to listen with incredulity when I told them." James Fennimore Cooper used a huge vocabulary in his adventure novel *The Last of the Mohicans*. In one of his sentences, Cooper wrote that "Magua shook his head incredulously."

One of the most famous sentences in all of English literature occurs in Charles Dickens's *A Tale of Two Cities*, in which Dickens described the French Revolution as "the epoch of incredulity." An epoch is an age, a period of years. Why do you think that Dickens would have called that period of great revolution an epoch of incredulity?

PERPLEX

The verb *perplex* comes from the Latin *perplexus*, in which *per* meant thoroughly, and *plexus* meant involved. Does *perplex* still mean thoroughly involved today? Usually, no. To perplex is to bewilder, confuse, or puzzle. The idea is that the perplexed person is lost, completely unable to grasp something or to think clearly about it. In his 1667 masterpiece *Paradise Lost*, John Milton wrote of "perplexing thoughts." In 1719 Daniel Defoe wrote in *Robinson Crusoe*, "And yet here I was perplexed again." Emily Brontë combined two of our words in a sentence of *Wuthering Heights*, when her character speaks "with a perplexed countenance." Frederick Douglass wrote in his great *Narrative* that "Our want of reverence for him must have perplexed him greatly." In *Tom Sawyer*, Mark Twain wrote that "The school stared in perplexity at this incredible folly." Many other great children's novels use this word; Robert Louis Stevenson used it in *Treasure Island* to describe "his face still wearing the expression of extreme perplexity." In Jack London's *The Call of the Wild*, we read that "The driver was perplexed." In Rouse's wonderful translation of *The Odyssey of*

Homer, we read that "Saying this she went down the stairs with a heart full of perplexity."

WHO IS THAT WRITER?

The English novelist Jane Austen wrote one of the most popular and influential novels of all time, *Pride and Prejudice*. Born in 1775 in Steventon, Hampshire, England, Austen wrote her first novel at the age of fourteen, and the bulk of her famous novels in her early twenties. Although she published numerous novels during her lifetime, no one knew it at first—she initially did not use her name, but only gave "By a Lady" as the author's identity. Jane Austen died in 1817 and is buried in Winchester Cathedral.

WHAT IS THIS WRITER SAYING?

Discuss the meaning of the **bold** word in each of the following sentences:

From Joseph Conrad's *Heart of Darkness*: "The swift and indifferent **placidity** of that look troubled me."

From Upton Sinclair's *The Jungle*: "Jurgis was no longer **perplexed** when he heard men talk of fighting for their rights."

From Rachel Carson's *Silent Spring*: "Our attitude toward plants is a **singularly** narrow one."

From Scott Fitzgerald's *The Great Gatsby*: "My **incredulity** was submerged into fascination now."

CAESAR'S WORD SEARCH

In the puzzle, find the Latin-based English words.

```
D I D S A P R E D I C T D B P S
I N E B U Q C I P Q M P N I O E
C C B M E P U N M U R S U P S E
A I R O A D E A A V B F O E T L
L S I A E L N R M L V E F R E B
P E E A V I A E A A R S O P R A
I D F F X C L D C N R N R L I T
A N T E R I O R R S N I P E O I
G R O T E S Q U E O E U N X R U
S U O L U D E R C N I D A E E Q
S I N G U L A R P S N T N T D E
P G P P R O S C R I B E D O E F
V D T N E V M U C R I C G O C D
S U O I G I D O R P D T O T N O
D S S U P E R F L U O U S U O V
L O N M A N I F E S T C O M C X
```

profound	aquamarine	superannuated	prelude
manifest	concede	superfluous	proscribed
prodigious	debrief	predict	serene
incised	grotesque	condescend	odious
circumvent	maladroit	posterior	equitable
anterior	placid	singular	amiable
incredulous	perplex		

1. Which of these words makes you think of poetry?
2. Which of these words might describe a pretty day?
3. Which of these words are powerful adjectives?
4. Which words rhyme or almost rhyme?
5. Can you use three of the words in one good sentence?

CAESAR'S GRAMMAR · PARTS OF SENTENCE

Study the first four examples, then try to do the second four the same way.

1. Octavian disgregarded his uncle's **singular** order.
      n.   v.   adj.   n.   adj.   n.
     subj.   AVP   D.O.
   Note: The direct object is a noun or pronoun that receives the action.

2. The **placid** ocean showed no hint of the coming storm.
   adj.   adj.   n.   v.   adj.   n. prep. adj.   adj.   n.
                subj.   AVP   D.O.

3. The decisive Caesar was not an **amiable** man.
   adj.   adj.   n.   v.   adv. adj.   adj.   n.
               subj.   LVP   S.C.

4. The **incredulous** crowd screamed insults at Antony.
   adj.   adj.   n.   v.   n.   prep.   n.
                   subj.   AVP   D.O.

5. The disciplined strategy **perplexed** the untrained barbarians.

6. The **audible** insult gave Caesar a moment of hesitation.

7. The conquered city was a **grotesque** and tragic scene.

8. The Celts despised the **odious** superiority of the Romans.

CAESAR'S SPANISH

Everywhere we turn, language reveals to us that modern English and modern Spanish share words from ancient Latin:

Latin	Spanish	English
placidus	plácido	placid
singularis	singular	singular
amicabilis	amable	amiable
incredulus	incrédulo	incredulous
perplexus	perplejo	perplex

CAESAR'S SYNONYMS

Here are words that are similar to the words in our list, but are they exactly the same in meaning or are they slightly different? For each word on our list, look up any synonym that you do not know, then pick one, and carefully explain the difference between it and our word.

placid: serene, calm, halcyon, peaceful, still, unruffled, even, quiet, unperturbed, impassive

singular: unique, particular, individual, differentiated, separate, discontinuous, discrete

amiable: genial, cordial, amicable, convivial, affable, sociable, friendly, personable, approachable

incredulous: doubting, questioning, skeptical, challenging, disbelieving, suspecting, uncertain, mistrustful

perplex: bewilder, baffle, confuse, mystify, befuddle, dumbfound, distract, stump, addle, stymie, muddle, elude

CAESAR'S ANTONYMS

For each of the words in this lesson, think of a word that is an antonym.

1. **placid**
2. **singular**
3. **amiable**
4. **incredulous**
5. **perplex**

Are there any words in this list that have no antonyms? Are there any for which it is difficult to think of an antonym? Why?

CAESAR'S ANALOGY

Analogies are about relationships. Find a second pair of words that have the same relationship to each other as the first pair has. Remember that it sometimes helps to put the two words into a sentence that makes the relationship clear.

MIRACLE : INCREDULOUS ::

a. placid : serene

b. singular : common

c. mystery : perplexed

d. allude : refer

THE SENATE CROWD

Michael Clay Thompson

The placid day had changed to blank despair,
and now the mob—perplexed—had gathered here,
before the Senate, staring at the stair
and clamoring, incredulous with fear.
Some hack, with maladroit and clichéd words,
—to him sublime, to us absurd—began
decrying loudly to the worried herd,
—I mean ourselves—about some odious plan.
"A murder cruel," he said, with countenance
distressed, and then *sub rosa* murmurs rose
amid the crowd in anger, and the glances
and the cries, the sudden loss of hope.
"It's Caesar," someone tremulously said.
"He's gone." Prodigious words—we turned and fled.

This poem is an English sonnet: three quatrains and a couplet, with the rhyme scheme being abab, cdcd, efef, gg. The meter is iambic pentameter. This time I did not put line spaces to reveal the quatrains and the couplet. I have used examples of near rhyme, such as the assonance in *rose/ hope*, rather than perfect rhyme, in some cases.

CAESAR'S PARAGRAPH

We have written a descriptive paragraph and a comparison paragraph. Now let us write an **expository** paragraph. As we learn from *Paragraph Town*, an expository paragraph is a paragraph that explains something, giving reasons.

Let us write a serious expository paragraph about why Rome was able to take control of the ancient Mediterranean world. Do some reading and collect some of the reasons for Rome's success, and then write a paragraph that explains why Rome was so powerful.

Work in as many of this lesson's five words as you can, and add others from previous lessons. As always, remember to use the vocabulary words correctly.

The paragraph can be long if you wish it to be. Remember to organize the sentences into a clear sequence so that they do not confuse the reader.

Remember that this paragraph should be academic writing—school writing—which means that you should not use first person (*I*, *me*) and you are not allowed to use contractions (*isn't*, *didn't*, *don't*). In other words, never mention yourself, and always write with complete words. Focus on facts; do not try to be cute or entertaining.

JULIUS CAESAR, PART VIII

On the Ides of March, March 15th, of 44 B.C., Julius Caesar left home to attend a session of the Senate to address matters prior to leaving for his invasion of Parthia. His cousin, Mark Antony, had heard a *sub rosa* rumor that when Caesar reached the Senate, there would be an attempt on his life by conspirators who feared Caesar's increasingly condescending power. The conspirators, knowing that Mark Antony might warn Caesar, arranged to delay and distract Antony to circumvent his interference.

Undeterred by the profound protests of his wife Calpurnia, who had suffered singular nightmares and begged Caesar to remain at home, Caesar arrived at the Senate and, after a moment's distraction by Cimber, was stabbed by conspirators including Cimber, Casca, Cassius, and Brutus. In a final gesture of dignity, Caesar pulled his toga over his own face as he died.

Although the unabashed Brutus and other conspirators left the grotesque scene and hurried to the Capitol maladroitly clamoring, "People of Rome, we are once again free," they found manifest silence in the streets because the perplexed citizens, discovering that something odious and dangerous was occurring, had withdrawn into their homes.

Caesar's assassination incited a series of wars and political disarray. Incredulous Roman common citizens were furious that a group of aristocratic conspirators had murdered Caesar. It was Caesar's grandnephew Octavian, only eighteen years old in 44 B.C., who would rise to power and change Rome from a republic to an empire with himself, now the Emperor Augustus Caesar, at its sublime head.

REVIEW FOR CUMULATIVE QUIZ VIII

bi	two	**dis**	away
sub	under	**sym**	together
de	down	**circum**	around
pre	before	**mal**	bad
super	over	**post**	after
un	not	**equi**	equal
inter	between	**ante**	before
semi	half		

bicameral	having two chambers	*sub rosa*	done in secret
debrief	to question someone	**preexist**	existing beforehand
superannuated	obsolete	**countenance**	facial expression
profound	deep	**manifest**	obvious
prodigious	huge	**languor**	weakness
unabashed	not embarrassed	**interdict**	a prohibition
semiannual	twice a year or half-yearly	**disarray**	disorganization or disorder
symbiotic	mutually beneficial	**serene**	calm
acute	sharp	**grotesque**	distorted
condescend	to patronize	**odious**	hateful
circumvent	get around	**maladroit**	clumsy, bungling
posterior	at the back, later	**equitable**	fair, impartial
anterior	near the front, earlier	**exquisite**	beautifully made
clamor	outcry	**sublime**	lofty
tremulous	quivering	**allude**	indirectly refer to
aquamarine	light bluish-green	**audible**	able to be heard
proscribed	forbidden	**concede**	surrender, admit defeat
incised	cut in	**placid**	calm
singular	unique	**amiable**	friendly
incredulous	skeptical	**perplex**	confuse

THE IONIAN COLUMN

Thomas Milton Kemnitz

The Ionian style was developed about a century after the Doric; its columns were slenderer with a height of about eight times the diameter of the base. The Ionian column sits on a base that raises it off the floor or platform; it has twenty-four parallel flutes as opposed to the twenty of the stouter Doric column; the *volute* at its top is named from the Latin *voluta,* meaning scroll. The total impact of the Ionian is of a much more elegant column, lighter, more decorated, soaring to sublime heights the Doric column does not reach. The Ionian column style was used for the White House in Washington, D.C.

LATIN STEMS · LESSON IX

stem	*meaning*	*modern examples*
cred	believe	incredulous, credo, credible
miss	send	missive, remiss, emission
cide	kill	regicide, homicide, fratricide
dict	say	edict, malediction, contradict
bell	war	rebellion, bellicose, belligerent

CRED means believe. When we cannot believe someone, we are *incredulous*. A *credo* (pronounced KREEdoe) is a set of beliefs, and something is *credible* when it is believable.

MISS means send. A *missive* is an official letter that you send. To be *remiss* in your duty means that we have to send you back to do it again, and an *emission* is like car exhaust that is sent out.

CIDE means kill. To kill a king is *regicide*. To kill a human is *homicide*, and to kill a brother is *fratricide*.

DICT means say. An *edict* is an official public statement that has the force of law. A *malediction* is a curse, and to *contradict* is to say something against another's statement.

BELL means war. A *rebellion* is a war of opposition. The adjective *bellicose* means extremely warlike, and *belligerent* is another adjective that means warlike and hostile.

itable submission fungicide
miss mission edict credence
ebellion addiction fratricide
ission manumission dictate
e predict emissary dictation
edibility insecticide creditor
le remission verdict dictum
cose credulity transmission
redo dictionary benediction
de commission incredulous
ssionary matricide genocide
issory accreditation indict
germicide creditable dictum
t belligerent missile suicide
ion microbicide valediction

NONFICTION WORDS

Here are five advanced nonfiction words. You will not hear them in daily conversation, but you will encounter them in your future academic life. Each word is based on one of the stems in this lesson.

stem	word	definition
cred	**credo**	a set of beliefs
miss	**emissary**	a messenger
cide	**regicide**	the killing of a king
dict	**edict**	an official order
bell	**antebellum**	from before the war

CREDO is a noun that refers to a set of beliefs. Someone might say, "I accept the credo of equality that Jefferson expressed in the *Declaration of Independence*."

EMISSARY is a noun that refers to a messenger or someone such as a diplomat who is sent out on a special mission. In *David Copperfield*, Charles Dickens describes "an emissary of the police."

REGICIDE is a noun that refers to the killing of a king, something that appears not only in history but also in great literature.

EDICT is a noun that refers to an official order or pronouncement by someone in authority. We often say that someone issues an edict. The novelist Pearl Buck referred to "sacred edicts."

ANTEBELLUM is an adjective that refers to a period before a war. In American English, this usually means before the Civil War. In his novel *All the King's Men*, Robert Penn Warren described "old papers and antebellum relics and keepsakes."

CAESAR'S ANALOGY

The first two words are related to each other in a special way. Is one before the other? Is one inside the other? Are they opposites? Find the pair below that has the same relationship as the first pair.

REGICIDE : HOMICIDE ::
    a. missive : communication
    b. incredulous : gullible
    c. friendly : furious
    d. malediction : blessing

ADVANCED WORD: BELLICOSE

The adjective *bellicose* (bell-ih-kose), from the Latin *bellicosus*, contains the stems *bell* (war) and *ose* (full of). *Bellicose* means really warlike, inclined to start quarrels or wars. In her great book about nature and the danger of chemical pesticides, *Silent Spring*, Rachel Carson wrote that honeybees that have contacted pesticides become "wildly agitated and bellicose." A good synonym for *bellicose* is the adjective *pugnacious*, which means wanting to fight.

ADVANCED WORD: INCREDULOUS

The adjective *incredulous* means full of disbelief. When we see something that is incredible, we feel incredulous. *Incredulous* has been a favorite literary word for the past two centuries. Jane Austen, in *Pride and Prejudice*, wrote that "Elizabeth looked at her sister with incredulous solicitude." *Incredulous* also was used by Mary Shelley in *Frankenstein*, by James Fennimore Cooper in *The Last of the Mohicans*, and by Charlotte Brontë, who wrote in

Jane Eyre, "You may look incredulous, if you please." In Kenneth Grahame's *The Wind in the Willows*, an event takes place "full in view of the astonished and hitherto incredulous Mole." In 1911 Frances Hodgson Burnett used *incredulous* in her novel *The Secret Garden*: "'Tha' doesn't want thy porridge.' Martha exclaimed incredulously." And in Gilbreth's classic *Cheaper by the Dozen*, we read, "'Are you crazy?' the husband asked incredulously." American novelist Toni Morrison, who was the first American woman to win the Nobel Prize for Literature since Pearl Buck won it in the 1920s, used *incredulous* in her novel *Song of Solomon*; she wrote that "Freddie was incredulous."

Which of these examples of *incredulous* do you like the best?

How many different meanings of *incredulous* do you see?

How many of these novels that use *incredulous* have you heard of before?

WHO IS THAT WRITER?

Toni Morrison was born in Lorain, Ohio, in 1931. Her work expresses both universal themes and the African-American experience in America and is filled with detailed observation and deep compassion. Morrison earned an M.A. degree in English at Cornell University in 1955 and taught at Texas Southern University and Howard University before becoming an editor at Random House, one of the major publishing firms. Her novels such as *Song of Solomon* and *Beloved* earned her the Nobel Prize for literature in 1993.

CAESAR'S WORD SEARCH

In the puzzle, find the Latin-based English words.

```
Y P O S T E R I O R Q M E L D C
P R E D I C T N E V M U C R I C
C R E D O P R O D I G I O U S I
E D E B I R C S O R P A R R F C
L E D S C E A N T E B E L L U M
B D S E U D M A N I F E S T M B
A I U U B O N I A X E L P R E P
T C P Q R R L E S N E D I C T T
I I E S E A I U C S T N P E I X
U G R E L A L E D S A E E O S N
Q E F T B D O U F E E R R R B M
E R L O A I D B G A R D Y I E C
F D U R I C I D Q N A C N A O S
L V O G M A O A I L I N N O D R
E Y U F A L U V A L I S I I C G
F T S M B P S M I N C I S E D G
```

manifest	concede	superfluous	proscribed
prodigious	debrief	predict	serene
incised	grotesque	condescend	odious
circumvent	maladroit	posterior	equitable
anterior	placid	singular	amiable
incredulous	perplex	credo	emissary
regicide	edict	antebellum	languor

1. Which of these words might be insulting?
2. Which of these words might be a compliment?
3. Which of these words are nouns?
4. Which words might be useful in talking about government?
5. Can you use three of the words in one good sentence?

CAESAR'S GRAMMAR · PARTS OF SENTENCE
Study the first four examples, and then try to do the second four the same way.

1. The imperial **edict** revealed a brutal and dictatorial **credo**.
   adj. adj. n. v. adj. adj. conj. adj. n.
   subj. AVP D.O.

2. Caesar's **emissary** gave the king a stern warning.
   n. n. v. adj. n. adj. adj. n.
   subj. AVP I.O. D.O.

3. The laws of the empire changed after the **regicide**.
   adj. n. prep. adj. n. v. prep. adj. adj.
   subj. AVP

4. The **antebellum** luxuries were now a thing of the past.
   adj. adj. n. v. adv. adj. n. prep. adj. n.
   subj. LVP S.C.

5. His **amiable** welcome did not fool the barbarian **emissary**.

6. Justinian was **incredulous** about the defeat of his legions.

7. The barbarians made **exquisitely** beautiful jewelry.

8. The **sublime** justice of **equitable** law impressed the tribe.

CAESAR'S SPANISH

stem	meaning	English / Spanish examples
cred	believe	incredulous / incrédulo
miss	send	missive / misivo
cide	kill	regicide / regicidio
dict	say	edict / edicto
bell	war	bellicose / belicoso

A ROMAN FACT

Lucius Annaeus Seneca, a Stoic philosopher, was born in what is now Spain in 4 B.C. He wrote that we should read philosophers, not just the outlines of philosophy—the full original works. He also told us that we should read good books many times, rather than many books. Why do you think he gave us that advice?

CAESAR'S MATHEMATICS

In a five-year period, Hadrian holds CDXXIII meetings with architects and engineers to discuss building walls and arches. He also holds XVII meetings about edicts he is considering, and he meets with LXXIII emissaries to give them their orders. How many meetings does Hadrian endure?

AFTERMATH

Michael Clay Thompson

When the cruel regicide was fomented,
an edict came forth from the state:
All protests proscribed for the moment.
All credos suspended posthaste.

All audible clamoring outlawed,
all chaotic antebellum disarray,
superseded by fixed interdiction:
No crowd may assemble today.

Then the high emissary departed,
and *sub rosa* grumblings arose,
but not manifestly imparted,
just whispered from doors that were closed.

Too bad for the dictator fallen,
Too bad for the loss of control—
our freedoms will never be hollowed;
this placidity's only a role.

Next year when the spring swells the rivers,
and the trees are beginning to green,
we'll teach them what tremulous shivers
come from equitable freedoms serene.

JULIUS CAESAR, PART IX

As we have seen, Caesar's assassination triggered a chain of events that eventually led to the end of the Roman republic and the establishment of an imperial state. After the odious news of Caesar's death was manifest in the city of Rome, Mark Antony, who wanted power, stirred the grotesque emotion of the crowds. Clamoring mobs attacked the homes of Brutus and Cassius. Caesar's body was cremated in a public ceremony, with people in disarray throwing branches and other combustible materials on his pyre until it burned part of the Forum.

To Mark Antony's profound incredulity, Caesar had named his grandnephew Octavian as his sole heir, and a complex series of civil wars followed. Antony first sided with Octavian against the forces of the assassins Brutus and Cassius, and with forty-five legions they defeated the militarily maladroit Brutus and Cassius at the battle of Philippi in eastern Macedonia in 42 B.C.

Antony then joined with the Egyptian queen Cleopatra VII, and they entered into a new civil war against Octavian, who defeated them in a naval battle in the Ionian Sea off of Actium on September 2, 31 B.C. With Octavian's triumph, he ascended to control of Rome, becoming the first Roman emperor with the name *Augustus Caesar*. We refer to him now as *Augustus*. Julius Caesar had been deified (regarded as a god) after his death, and Augustus enjoyed the same credo, being known as *Divi Filius*, the son of a god.

Augustus ruled the prodigious Roman empire from 27 B.C. until 14 A.D. Under his edicts, Rome established the placid Pax Romana, a singular 200-year era of peace in the Mediterranean.

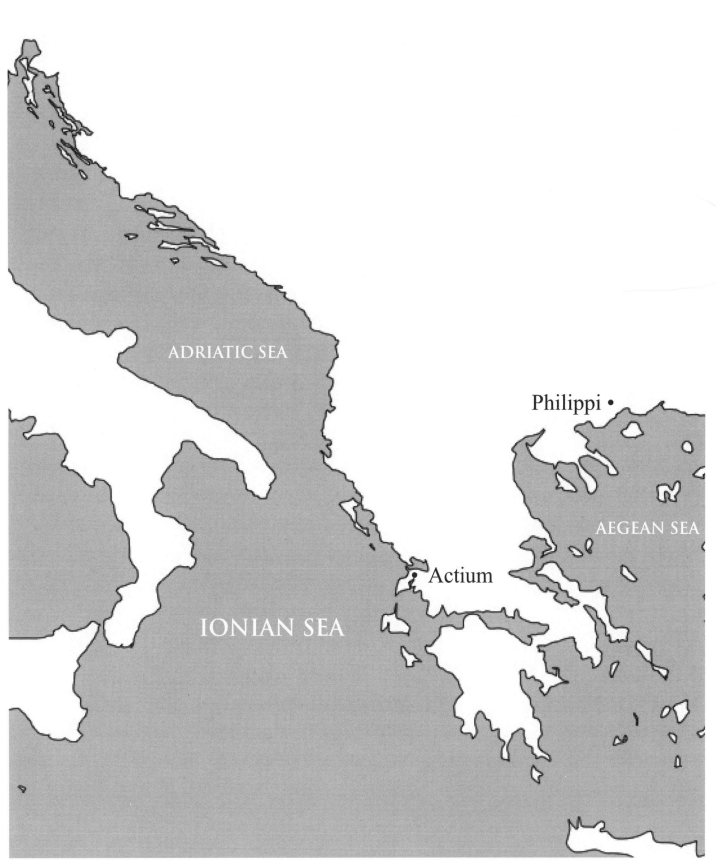

ADRIATIC SEA

Philippi •

AEGEAN SEA

Actium

IONIAN SEA

REVIEW FOR CUMULATIVE QUIZ IX

bi	two	**dis**	away
sub	under	**sym**	together
de	down	**circum**	around
pre	before	**mal**	bad
super	over	**post**	after
un	not	**equi**	equal
inter	between	**ante**	before
semi	half	**cred**	believe
miss	send	**cide**	kill
dict	say	**bell**	war

bicameral	having two chambers	*sub rosa*	done in secret
debrief	to question someone	**preexist**	existing beforehand
superannuated	obsolete	**countenance**	facial expression
profound	deep	**manifest**	obvious
prodigious	huge	**languor**	weakness
unabashed	not embarrassed	**interdict**	a prohibition
semiannual	twice a year or half-yearly	**disarray**	disorganization or disorder
symbiotic	mutually beneficial	**serene**	calm
acute	sharp	**grotesque**	distorted
condescend	to patronize	**odious**	hateful
circumvent	get around	**maladroit**	clumsy, bungling
posterior	at the back, later	**equitable**	fair, impartial
anterior	near the front, earlier	**exquisite**	beautifully made
clamor	outcry	**sublime**	lofty
tremulous	quivering	**allude**	indirectly refer to
aquamarine	light bluish-green	**audible**	able to be heard
proscribed	forbidden	**concede**	surrender, admit defeat
incised	cut in	**placid**	calm
singular	unique	**amiable**	friendly
incredulous	skeptical	**perplex**	confuse
credo	a set of beliefs	**emissary**	a messenger
regicide	the killing of a king	**edict**	an official order
antebellum	from before the war		

THE CORINTHIAN COLUMN

Thomas Milton Kemnitz

The Corinthian column is more elegant than the Ionian; the column can be more slender with a nine-to-one ratio rather than the eight to one of the Ionian column. It has the same twenty-four parallel incised flutes of the Ionian column, but the Corinthian column is topped by a much higher, more elaborate header. Several—usually four—layers of acanthus leaves are topped by twin scrolls. The Corinthian style was developed a century later than the Ionian style, and it was not extensively used until the Roman emperors favored it four centuries later for their public buildings. Hadrian's arch in Athens and the Pantheon in Rome (pictured below) were built using the Corinthian style, as was the temple Hadrian built to Zeus pictured on the left, also in Athens.

CLASSIC WORDS · LESSON X

1. **melancholy**: sadness
2. **visage**: the face
3. **venerate**: to respect
4. **abate**: to lessen
5. **repose**: resting

MELANCHOLY

The English noun *melancholy* comes from the Latin *melancholia*, which came from the ancient Greek *mela*, black, and *chole*, bile. The idea was that sadness or dejection is caused by an excess of black bile in the body—something that we now know is not true. The idea, however, has survived in the word. *Melancholy* is an old word in English literature. Chaucer used it as far back as 1385, saying that the "humour of malencolye causeth ful many a man in sleep to crye." William Shakespeare used it in many of his plays. In *As You Like It,* written in 1599, he wrote that "The melancholy Jacques grieves at that." In his 1601 masterpiece *Hamlet*, the villainous uncle Claudius notes of Prince Hamlet that "There's something in his soul, o'er which his melancholy sits on brood." In Jonathan Swift's 1726 *Gulliver's Travels*, Gulliver says that "I rose up with as melancholy a disposition as ever I had in my life." In Lewis Carroll's 1865 story *Alice in Wonderland*, we read that "she had put the Lizard in head downwards, and the poor little thing was waving its tail about in a melancholy way." In Robert Louis Stevenson's *Treasure Island*, written in 1881, we read about "the look of the island, with its grey, melancholy woods." In Jack London's 1903 *The Call of the Wild*, there is "the melancholy rippling of waves on lonely beaches." We can see from these famous uses of the word that *melancholy* can describe a person's feelings, but it also can describe things in the environment that seem sad, or that make us feel sad. One of the most striking *melancholy* sentences comes from 1904, from James M. Barrie's great *Peter Pan*: "His eyes were of the blue of the forget-me-not, and of a profound melancholy."

VISAGE

The English noun *visage* is a synonym of our friend *countenance*. Perhaps there is a difference in emphasis in the words, with *countenance* focusing on the contents of the expression and *visage* emphasizing the look of the face; after all, *visage* traces back to the Latin *videre*, to see. Even so, the two words both refer to the appearance of the face, and *countenance* often is used to define *visage*. We see from literature that the visage can be pale, comely, plump, or doleful. It can be domineering or stern. Chaucer described a "sad visage," and Shakespeare wrote a wonderful description of a mask in *Romeo and Juliet*: "Give me a case" he wrote, "to put my visage in." In *Paradise Lost*, the greatest epic poem in the English language, John Milton wrote of "Celestial visages," a "visage all inflamed," and a "visage incompos'd." In Sir Walter Scott's knight novel *Ivanhoe*, we read of the "scars with which is visage was seamed." And in Mary Shelley's *Frankenstein*, the poor monster explains that "I travelled only at night, fearful of encountering the visage of a human being." In James Fennimore Cooper's *The Last of the Mohicans*, we encounter "the scowling visage of Chingachgook." One of the greatest *visage* sentences comes from the great English novelist Charles Dickens, who in *A Tale of Two Cities* described someone's "taciturn and ironbound visage." *Taciturn* means silent, and so this character's visage is frozen and metallic—not very pleasant.

VENERATE

To *venerate* is to respect or revere, to admire. The word traces all the way back to the Roman's word *venus*, love. *Veneration* is a kind of high, respectful love. The adjective form of the word is *venerable*. It is important for many words to see that they are available in different parts of speech: *venerate* is a verb, *veneration* is a noun, *venerable* is an adjective. Being able to change forms like this gives a word great power in our sentences. What kinds of things can we venerate? What things can be venerable? In British and American literature, there are venerable white beards, venerable towns, venerable bows of ships, and venerable friends. We often use *venerable* to describe what is religious; there are venerable ministers, venerable pastors, and venerable chapels. In *Walden*, Henry David Thoreau wrote of a "venerable moss-grown and hoary ruin." In *Song of Myself*, part of his great *Leaves of Grass*, Walt Whitman asked, "Why should I venerate and be ceremonious?" Sometimes veneration is very sincere; in *Uncle Tom's Cabin*, Harriet Beecher Stowe described a character who was "gazing upward with a face fervent with veneration." The word *fervent* means that the face was very intense, very sincere. In Sir Walter Scott's *Ivanhoe*, we also see this kind of earnest veneration; another character had extended "his hand to Gurth, who kissed it with the utmost possible veneration." In *Gulliver's Travels*, Jonathan Swift had his main character Gulliver admit that "I have too great a veneration for crowned heads." In Charlotte Brontë's great novel *Jane Eyre*, Jane confesses that "I deeply venerated my cousin's talent and principle."

ABATE

Our English verb *abate* means to lessen in amount or degree, but it comes from the Old French *abattre*, to beat down. This, in turn, came from the Latin *batuere*, to beat. Writers have used *abate* to describe how things go down, reduce, or recede. Note that in order for something to get smaller, it must first be bigger, and so *abate* is what big things do. Big storms abate. Big emotions abate. In Bram Stoker's *Dracula,* we read, "When the snow storm abated we looked again." In Kingston's translation of Wyss's *The Swiss Family Robinson*, we read that "Toward evening the universal excitement began to abate, and the party assembled for supper with tolerable composure." In Robert Louis Stevenson's *Kidnapped*, we read that "my strength had much abated." In Scott's *Ivanhoe*, we are relieved to learn that "His fever is abated." Mary Shelley, in *Frankenstein*, wrote that "I continued with unabated fervour to traverse immense deserts." This is a great sentence for us to study because it contains not only the negative of *abate*, but it also contains *traverse*, another verb in this book. *Traverse* means cross, and so traversing a desert is crossing it. In Shakespeare's great tragedy, *King Lear*, the pitiful old king complains that his daughter has gotten rid of his train, his group of servants: "She hath abated me of half my train," he cries.

REPOSE

The English word *repose* traces all the way back to the Latin *pausa*, to pause. When we re-pose, we pause again. When we use *repose* as a verb, it means the act of resting, and when we use *repose* as a noun, it refers to rest. In Shakespeare's 1611 play *The Tempest*, a character sleepwalks: "This is a strange repose, to be asleep with eyes wide open—standing, speaking, moving, and yet so fast asleep." Two hundred hears after Shakespeare, Mary Shelley used *repose* in *Frankenstein* to paint a picture of tranquility: "all nature reposed under the eye of the quiet moon." In *The Legend of Sleepy Hollow*, Washington Irving wrote that "A small brook glides through it, with just murmur enough to lull one to repose." An interesting use comes from Sir Walter Scott in *Ivanhoe*, where the knights take the trouble "to repose their horses." Robert Louis Stevenson used *repose* in *Dr. Jekyll and Mr. Hyde* to describe the repose of an inanimate (mindless) object: "he locked the note into his safe, where it reposed from that time forward." In Frances Hodgson Burnett's *The Secret Garden* there is "a new reposeful sleep." In Kenneth Grahame's *The Wind in the Willows* there is a "well-earned repose." And in George Orwell's *Animal Farm* ,"Napoleon reposed on a bed of straw." Napoleon, being a pig, needed his repose.

repose

CAESAR'S WORD SEARCH

In the puzzle, find the Latin-based English words.

```
E E N E R E S D E S I C N I Y G
D Y F E L B A I M A T C I D E G
I R E P O S E E E M I S S A R Y
C X E D D F L A N G U O R I V E
I V Q I S U O L U D E R C N I U
G E U C A Y M A L A D R O I T Q
E N I A G S B F R Y T S F O A S
R E T L Y A U A L N U E A N E E
E R A P T Q L O E O I H T G G T
N A B E F U H V I R E E A T X O
C T L R G C M D B G R S P C E R
R E E N N U O E O I I H T I L G
E D I A C Q D H O V P D N D P M
D S L R S L A R N S R R O E R H
O E I R O I R E T S O P C R E N
M C T D N E C S E D N O C P P D
```

prodigious	debrief	predict	serene
incised	grotesque	condescend	odious
circumvent	maladroit	posterior	equitable
anterior	placid	singular	amiable
incredulous	perplex	credo	emissary
regicide	edict	repose	languor
melancholy	visage	venerate	abate

1. Which of these words conveys the most emotion?
2. Which of these words might describe a friend?
3. Which of these words are verbs?
4. Which words might be useful in talking about the ocean?
5. Can you use three of the words in one good sentence?

CAESAR'S GRAMMAR · PARTS OF SENTENCE

Study the first four examples and then try to do the second four the same way.

1. The   crowd   in   the   street   was   **melancholy**.
   adj.   n.   prep. adj.   n.   v.   adj.
        subj.   LVP   S.C.

2. The emperor's stern **visage** intimidated the barbarian emissary.
   adj.   n.   adj.   n.   v.   adj.   adj.   n.
                 subj.   AVP   D.O.

3. The citizens **venerated** Caesar more after his assassination.
   adj.   n.   v.   n.   adv.   prep. adj.   n.
        subj.   AVP   D.O.

4. By early morning the storm over the city **abated**.
   prep. adj.   n.   adj.   n.   prep. adj. n.   v.
                     subj.   AVP
   Note: There is not always a direct object when there is an action verb. Sometimes nothing receives the action.

5. The new treaty initiated a period of political **repose**.

6. The harsh **edict proscribed** all criticism of the emperor.

7. The site of the **prodigious** battle was Philippi in Macedonia.

8. The elite troops moved from the **posterior** lines to the front.

IN BRITAIN, MOVING NORTH

Michael Clay Thompson

An emissary sent from Rome arrived
and caused clamor among the officers.
We knew not what was up. Some said
a new edict was eminent. And yessiree,
next morning here they came. "Prepare
to march. One hour. That's all you have.
Assemble there within the palisade,"
with visage stern. We knew the drill.
By mid-day dust was rising from our tread,
and tramping north we left the fort behind.
"Suppress the rebel disarray," they said.
Oh right. *You* try to catch those guys
who hide behind the trees and throw
their rocks and shoot their bows. Flies,
that's just the sound they make. And while
by sunset we were miles away, at ease,
constructing camp and cooking vittles vile,
somewhere up there, among the trees,
we heard *sub rosa* whispers, phony birds.
You're not alone, it meant. We hear your every word.
Our discipline did not abate the drift of dread.
We fight in open fields. It's how we're bred,
but not this cowardly guerilla stuff.
A sense of melancholy is a rough
beginning to a fight. Our night repose

was minimal, by first light. We would concede
that Rome must stamp rebellions out,
but how can we fight shouts from shadows,
missiles sent from trees, and spears and arrows
of outrageous forces? It's against the rules
of war, these sneaking bombards—shots of fools—
and they should be proscribed, unmanly acts
of war. We're Roman legions, trained to fight
in tight formation, not with hiding guys
who circumvent the rules we know. So now
we've broken camp and stamp stamp stamp
we march ahead, our credo firm, the boughs
of trees on either side are tremulous
with moving enemies who snap and birdcall
all they want. We march incredulous
at all their maladroit hijinks, appalling
tactics—antebellum amateurs, to us.
But now a darker forest up ahead
is looming—small the middle path that thins
into its shadows odious, and close
the trees. We do not like the looks of this.
And "Halt," the new commander hisses.
Then from the posterior ranks the scouts
come riding up. "Go in there," says he, placidly,
as though it were a picnic, so serene.
And in they go. We wait. We strain and lean,
but cannot hear the horses' hooves.

One technique in this poem is that it is enjambed. This means that often there are not periods or commas at the ends of the lines. We do not stop reading at the ends of enjambed lines. We read right through as though it were a prose paragraph. The enjambment conceals rhymes.

JULIUS CAESAR, PART X

To think of Rome is to think of Caesar. There are many great figures in the history of Rome, but the very name *Caesar* has become synonymous with leadership; manifestations of his name—such as *Kaiser*, *Tsar*, and *Qaysar*—persist around the world as titles of supreme rulers. From Augustus to Hadrian, Rome itself used Caesar's name in the titles of its emperors.

Two thousand years after Caesar's death, the Western world still uses (with a slight variation from Pope Gregory XIII) the Julian calendar that Caesar ordered, with the month of July referring to Julius Caesar himself. Prior to Caesar's revision of the superannuated Roman calendar, July, which was the month Caesar was born, was named *Quintilis*. The other names of the months also allude to Roman culture, such as *January* for the god Janus, *March* for the god Mars, *May* for the goddess Maia, *June* for Juno, and *August* for Augustus Caesar. September, October, November, and December refer to Roman numbers: *septem*, *octo*, *novem*, and *decem*.

With his acute and aggressive mind, Caesar was formidable, if not amiable. Plain of visage, he was an imperfect genius of both war and politics, but his edicts brought an end to the disarray of the Roman republic and its maladroit oligarchy, consolidating into his own hands the profound resources of the state. After Caesar, Roman emperors had the power they needed to defend and extend the empire, and this enabled Greco-Roman culture, which might have abated, to influence the West for hundreds of years after Caesar's death. Had it not been for Caesar, the Western world might not have the Greco-Roman foundation that it has today.

REVIEW FOR CUMULATIVE QUIZ X

bi	two	**dis**	away
sub	under	**sym**	together
de	down	**circum**	around
pre	before	**mal**	bad
super	over	**post**	after
un	not	**equi**	equal
inter	between	**ante**	before
semi	half	**cred**	believe
miss	send	**cide**	kill
dict	say	**bell**	war

bicameral	having two chambers	*sub rosa*	done in secret
debrief	to question someone	**preexist**	existing beforehand
superannuated	obsolete	**countenance**	facial expression
profound	deep	**manifest**	obvious
prodigious	huge	**languor**	weakness
unabashed	not embarrassed	**interdict**	a prohibition
semiannual	twice a year or half-yearly	**disarray**	disorganization or disorder
symbiotic	mutually beneficial	**serene**	calm
acute	sharp	**grotesque**	distorted
condescend	to patronize	**odious**	hateful
circumvent	get around	**maladroit**	clumsy, bungling
posterior	at the back, later	**equitable**	fair, impartial
anterior	near the front, earlier	**exquisite**	beautifully made
clamor	outcry	**sublime**	lofty
tremulous	quivering	**allude**	indirectly refer to
aquamarine	light bluish-green	**audible**	able to be heard
proscribed	forbidden	**concede**	surrender, admit defeat
incised	cut in	**placid**	calm
singular	unique	**amiable**	friendly
incredulous	skeptical	**perplex**	confuse
credo	a set of beliefs	**emissary**	a messenger
regicide	the killing of a king	**edict**	an official order
antebellum	from before the war	**melancholy**	sadness
visage	the face	**venerate**	to respect
abate	to lessen	**repose**	resting

THE TUSCAN COLUMN

Thomas Milton Kemnitz

Vitruvius dedicated his book on architecture to Augustus, and for the Emperor, nothing but the best would do. However, for a merchant in a provincial village like Herculaneum, there was always a temptation to do without some of the costly ornamentation inherent in the Greek style. Vitruvius noted in passing that there was a rustic style, but he did not elaborate on it. Some 1,600 years later, Renaissance authors—in an attempt to impose order upon a chaotic world—would identify this style as the Tuscan order. This tradition often built using smooth columns with plain capitals and bases.

The Roman use of brick enabled them to construct columns far easier than the Greeks who had to hue each column from stone or marble. Curved bricks made the construction of these columns particularly easy. They could build the column in bricks and mortar and then cover their outsides in a rendering of concrete.